MEDIEVAL REPRESENTATIVE INSTITUTIONS

Their Origins and Nature

Thomas N. Bisson
University of California, Berkeley

The Dryden Press
901 North Elm Street
Hinsdale, Illinois 60521

Copyright ©1973 by The Dryden Press
All Rights Reserved
Library of Congress Catalog Card Number: 73-75785
ISBN: 0-03-085285-4
Printed in the United States of America
345 090 987654321

Cover Credit:
Detail from a miniature in the *Actes du Procès de Robert d'Artois*
Bibliothèque Nationale, Paris

Contents

MEDIEVAL REPRESENTATIVE INSTITUTIONS

House of Lords under Edward I. Bettmann Archive.

Introduction

The rise of representative institutions is a celebrated fact of medieval European history. Rulers taking counsel with or asking consent of subjects who were becoming wealthier, more socially diverse, and better associated during the twelfth and thirteenth centuries created precedents for those recurrent assemblies of men from the several classes of society that flourished almost everywhere in Christian Europe from about 1250 to 1450. And it was in the parliaments, Estates, diets and Cortes of this "restless, assembly-loving age"[1] where were defined many of the deliberative practices that have persisted in the representative institutions of modern liberal-democratic societies. The uniqueness of the medieval evolution is not in doubt; historians agree that the circumstances and forms of European representation bear little resemblance to those known in antecedent or non-European societies. But if that is true, one is led to wonder why and how parliamentary institutions originated in Europe, and on these questions, as will appear, scholarly agreement has been conspicuously lacking. Closely related if not quite identical is the question of how the incipient representative bodies functioned. This issue, more intensively studied than the problem of origins, has especially exercised scholars interested in the parliament of England. Finally, historians have tried to explain why, except in England, parliamentarism declined before more or less absolute regimes after the fifteenth century. Concerning these broad problems—the origins, nature, and persistence (or demise) of representative institutions—this book is designed to illuminate the first two, which, unlike the third,[2] are problems in medieval history alone.

François Guizot and his younger contemporary, William Stubbs, were among the ablest nineteenth-century scholars to study medieval representative institutions. Their interpretations were deeply influenced by their own political ideals, posing the problem for subsequent workers of how to avoid anachronism in the description of past institutions. While both were fascinated by the English parliament, both could take broadly comparative views of the historical background of parliament, a permanently useful aspect of their work. The reader should also observe their common stress on the rise of the urban estate.

Stubbs' conception of the medieval parliament as a concentration of local communities brought to political maturity and coordination by a statesmanlike Edward I was a landmark in what soon became a torrent of specialized studies on the English institution. Stubbs had been an editor of narrative texts, the sources par excellence of political history; it was left to an editor and specialist in legal documents, F. W. Maitland, to show in 1893 that the form of early parliamentary records suggested that the judicial work of the king's council was more fundamental to parliament under Edward I than any political or legislative functions.

As the nineteenth century ended, the question of the nature—even "essence," as some later scholars spoke of it[3]—of the medieval parliament was so vigorously posed that it has continued to attract the ablest specialists ever since. The question of origins—that is, of how the Edwardian parliament came to assume its form and functions—seemed less controversial, and was often dealt with as an aspect of the "nature" of parliament. Thus, Désiré Pasquet, taking up a line of research pioneered by the German Ludwig Riess, regarded the summons of deputies from the shires and towns as a work of administrative necessity, thereby arriving at a conception of parliament altogether at variance with that favored by the Victorians. On the other hand, his stress on representation and on the "origins of the House of Commons," to quote his title, not only perpetuated an older perspective but tended again, however unwittingly, to illuminate the medieval parliament in a modern light.

The first scholars to set themselves resolutely against all taint of anachronism were H. G. Richardson and G. O. Sayles, who did much of their work in collaboration. Specializing in the early rolls of parliament, they came, not surprisingly, to conclusions reminiscent of Maitland's about the role of the council and the primacy of justice in early parliaments. But they went further. Testing evidence of all kinds, they tried to determine how contemporaries regarded parliaments as related to great councils and other kinds of meetings. In an early essay, Mr. Richardson employed the comparative method to show the resemblance of the early English parliament to the nascent Parlement of Paris, which was undoubtedly a tribunal.[4] And in that connection as in others he and Professor Sayles have emphasized that the histories of parliament and of representation should not be confused.

The work of Bertie Wilkinson, beginning in the 1930s, has resulted in further revision and even a revival of the "political" interpretation of the early English parliament. But Professor Wilkinson is not, or not simply, a neo-Stubbsian; he employs new concepts, works over the whole range of evidence, takes careful account of recent scholarship, and tries to distinguish between phases in the history of parliament during the first century of its existence.

Meanwhile, French scholars were busy with the history of the representative institutions known as "Estates" that developed in medieval France. But the conditions of discussion, and therefore the results, were very different from those in England. For everyone knew that France was a much larger country, in which not one but many assemblies arose; and that, with few exceptions, these bodies failed to preserve the rights that distinguished the English parliament in modern times. Moreover, the scholars who set out to investigate the Estates, one by one, tended to adhere to an orthodoxy, illustrated below in the selection from Joseph Billioud and criticized in those by Dupont-Ferrier and Émile Lousse, which was established in the later nineteenth century when parliamentarist ideals were still creating historical images. The reader should try to determine what questions underlie Billioud's account of the early Estates of Burgundy, and to compare them with those of the English scholars excerpted in the preceding section. To illustrate historical writing on the "Estates General, " selections have been taken from the works of C. H. McIlwain and Robert Fawtier, both distinguished scholars of the last generation. McIlwain's most famous study, *The High Court of Parliament and its Supremacy* . . . (1910), elaborated on Maitland's interpretation of parliament; his chapter on "Medieval Estates," here excerpted, stresses the progress of representation in a somewhat old-fashioned yet characteristically discerning way.

The recognition that parliamentary institutions had to be explained as an international phenomenon of the later Middle Ages was emphatically revived after the First World War. Marc Bloch's contribution, though very brief (he was not a specialist in this field), perceptively relates defects in the prevailing understanding of the origins of Estates to the parochial outlook of their historians. Robert Fawtier, on the other hand, continuing to salute the institutionalist understanding of Estates and, therefore, to ignore the more general problems of origins or causation,[5] offers a shrewd analysis of the Estates General in comparison with the English parliament.

If national or local studies have continued to focus on the nature or function of early parliamentary institutions, recent efforts to reexamine the field comparatively have revived the problem of explaining their origins. To Émile Lousse, it seemed necessary to call into question the entire conception of French and English historians, the "parliamentarists," as he termed them. Instead of studying assemblies, he urged, historians should investigate the societies, and social transformations, of which assemblies were but the expression. Lousse derived his "corporatist" theory from German scholarship, and his numerous studies, notably *La société d'Ancien Régime*,[6] helped to make it the prevailing, though never exclusive, theme of the International Commission for the History of Representative and Parliamentary Institutions, which published many articles and books by European historians after 1935.

More original if less revolutionary was the contribution of the American Gaines Post. In two remarkable articles published in 1943, Post argued that legal ideas derived from the revived Roman law explained much that was novel and important in the rise of representation. His main points are summarized in the general statement that prefaces the selection given below, although the remainder of that article is limited to the problem of the Roman-law proctor, and his powers, in southern Europe. In the study not included here, Post suggested that royal demands for "full powers" (*plena potestas*) from deputies to French and English assemblies toward 1300, indicative of the basically judicial form of Edward I's parliaments or Philip the Fair's assemblies, meant that consent in those bodies was formal, or "procedural," not sovereign or democratic (that is, not capable of being withheld).[7]

With Antonio Marongiu the stress on assemblies themselves has been revived. His work recalls an old debate among French historians[8] that was dropped in favor of the orthodoxy that understood representation only in terms of the rights of assemblies; yet his account of "pre-parliaments" and "true parliaments" may cause the reader to wonder whether Marongiu himself is not renewing the concept of pre-historic (that is, negligible) assemblies. G. I. Langmuir and T. N. Bisson, likewise dealing with very early assemblies, prefer to emphasize the governing concepts— notably counsel and aid—behind these bodies, which they tend to regard less as institutions than as occasions. Brian Tierney, sharing Gaines Post's perception of the influence of legal thought, proposes the novel solutions of ecclesiastical government as an explanation for the rise of secular "constitutionalism." His stress on consent is in an old but resilient tradition of scholarly understanding.

Needless to say, the present selection cannot pretend to cover the subject, nor even the debatable ground of the subject, of medieval representative institutions. Among important issues here excluded may be cited that of when the commons came to hold a necessary place among the estates of the English parliament, and that of the significance of taxation as a matter of consultation. In unusually persuasive studies, Professors C. H. Taylor and J. R. Strayer have argued that the large assemblies of the later thirteenth and fourteenth centuries, parliaments or Estates or otherwise, often functioned as devices to influence public opinion in quite novel circumstances.[9] Nor has it been possible to include material relating to the Empire or Italy, to say nothing of many other realms in which parliamentary bodies developed. It is hoped that readers will find compensation for these omissions in the emphasis on two or three of the regions where the history of early parliamentarism has flourished as vigorously in modern scholarship as in medieval practice.

A brief selection of original texts is appended, not so much to provide proofs of scholarly positions (far more space would be necessary for that) as to create some added perspective, some sense of "first handedness," to enliven the reading. These texts may be read in conjunction with the selections from secondary writing, where they are often cited, or separately as a chronological series of glimpses into the evolution of medieval ideas and practices of consultation.

One further observation is appropriate. Since historians generally "debate" in their studies and not before live audiences, their arguments do not always meet head on. The reader may be disconcerted by this difficulty in the present book. Yet the discussion is not necessarily the worse—at least, not less interesting—for its careening course. The important thing is to inquire what exactly an author seeks to show and to read critically for basic assumptions and "styles of thought" as well as for specific arguments. It is hoped that the reader may thereby find here the materials with which to draw conclusions of his own about a major subject of history.

Notes

1. E. P. Cheyney, *The Dawn of a New Era, 1250-1453* (New York, 1936), p. 87.
2. On the third, however, see pp. 78-83.
3. See, e.g., pp. 34, 41 ff.; and for criticism, J. G. Edwards, *Historians and the Medieval English Parliament* (Glasgow, 1960).
4. "The Origins of Parliament," *Transactions of the Royal Historical Society*, 4th ser., XI (1928), 137-183.
5. Fawtier could not conceive of royal assemblies other than as "controlling" (i.e., limiting) the monarchy, a perspective which effectively eliminated convocations prior to the fourteenth century from his understanding of parliamentarism. See R. Fawtier and F. Lot, *Histoire des institutions françaises* II (Paris, 1958), 545-577.
6. "Old Regime Society" (Louvain, 1943; 2d ed., 1952).
7. "*Plena Potestas* and Consent in Medieval Assemblies: a Study in Romano-Canonical Procedure and the Rise of Representation, 1150-1325," *Traditio*, I (1943), 355-408. On the point here mentioned, Post was countering J. G. Edwards, "The *Plena Potestas* of English Parliamentary Representatives," *Oxford Essays in Medieval History presented to H. E. Salter* (Oxford, 1934).
8. See A. Callery, "Les premiers États Généraux: origine, pouvoirs et attributions," *Revue de Questions Historiques*, XXIX (1881); cf. A. Luchaire, in *Annales de la Faculté des Lettres de Bordeaux*, III-IV (1881-1882).
9. J. R. Strayer and C. H. Taylor, *Studies in Early French Taxation* (Cambridge, M., 1939); J. R. Strayer, "The Statute of York and the Community of the Realm," *American Historical Review*, XLVII (1941), 1-22.

Part One   NINETEENTH CENTURY PERSPECTIVES

Chapter 1 EUROPEAN HISTORY AS THE HISTORY OF REPRESENTATIVE INSTITUTIONS

To FRANÇOIS GUIZOT (1787-1874),
among the foremost historians and statesmen of his day, the rise of representative
government seemed almost synonymous
with the history of Europe. He was professor
at the University of Paris when he gave the
famous lectures (1822) from which the
following excerpt is taken; later he served
the July Monarchy (1830-1848) in many
capacities, retiring on its collapse to resume
his voluminous historical writing. His
breadth of vision and liberal assumptions
evoke the enthusiasm with which scholars
began to inquire seriously into the origins of
parliamentary institutions.

[We] shall attempt to consider the ancient political institutions of Europe, and to sketch their history. While for this purpose we appropriate such lights as our age can furnish, we shall endeavour to carry with us none of the passions which divide it. . . . A system which evidently, from a general view of the subject, adheres continually to the same principles, starts from the same necessities, and tends to the same results, manifests or proclaims its presence throughout the whole of Europe. Almost everywhere the representative form of government is demanded, allowed, or established. This fact is, assuredly, neither an accident, nor the symptom of a transient madness. It has certainly its roots in the past political career of the nations, as it has its motives in their present condition. And if, warned by this, we turn our attention to the past, we shall everywhere meet with attempts, more or

From François Guizot, *History of the Origin of Representative Government in Europe*, tr. Andrew R. Scoble (London: Bohn's Standard Library, 1861), pp. 10-16 (abridged).

less successful, either made with a conscious regard to this system so as to produce it naturally, or striving to attain it by the subjugation of contrary forces. England, France, Spain, Portugal, Germany and Sweden supply us with numerous illustrations of this. . . .

We do not then, gentlemen, make an arbitrary choice, but one perfectly natural and necessary, when we make the representative form of government the central idea and aim of our history of the political institutions of Europe. To regard them from this point of view will not only give to our study of them the highest interest, but will enable us rightly to enter into the facts themselves, and truly to appreciate them. We shall then make this form of government the principal object of our consideration. We shall seek it wherever it has been thought to be discernible, wherever it has attempted to gain for itself a footing, wherever it has fully established itself. We shall inquire if it has in reality existed at times and in places where we have been accustomed to look for its germs. Whenever we find any indications of it, however crude and imperfect they may be, we shall inquire how it has been produced, what has been the extent of its power, and what influences have stifled it and arrested its progress. Arriving at last at the country where it has never ceased to consolidate and extend itself, from the thirteenth century to our own times, we shall remain there[1] in order to follow it in its march, to unravel its vicissitudes, to watch the development of the principles and institutions with which it is associated, penetrating into their nature and observing their action,—to study, in a word, the history of the representative system in that country where it really possesses a history which identifies itself with that of the people and their government. . . .

The history of the political institutions of Europe divides itself into four general epochs, during which society has been governed according to modes and forms essentially distinct. . . . [i.e., Germanic tribalism; secondly, the "feudal system," which] prevailed until the thirteenth century.

Then commenced a new epoch. The feudal lord, already possessed of royal power, aspired after royal dignity. A portion of the inhabitants of the territory, having regained somewhat of the power they had lost, longed to become free. The feudal aristocracy was attacked on the one hand by the enfranchisement of the townsmen and tenants, on the other hand by the extension of the royal power. Sovereignty tended to concentration, liberty to diffusion;—national unity began to shape itself at the same time as monarchical unity appeared. This was at once indicated and promoted by attempts after a representative form of government, which were made and renewed during nearly three centuries, wherever the feudal system fell into decay, or the monarchical system prevailed. But soon sovereigns also began almost everywhere to distrust it in their turn. They could not behold with indifference that sovereignty, which after having been long diffused had been regained and concentrated by their efforts, now again divided at its very centre. Besides, the people were deficient alike in such strength and knowledge as would enable them to continue, on the one hand, against the feudal system, a struggle which had not yet ceased, and to sustain, on the other hand, a new struggle against the central power. It was evident that the times were not fully matured; that society, which had not thoroughly emerged from that condition of servitude which had been the successor of social chaos, was neither so firmly consolidated nor so mentally disciplined as to be able to secure at once order by the equitable administration of power, and liberty by the safeguards of large and influential public institutions. The efforts after representative government became more occasional and feeble, and at length disappeared. One country alone guarded and defended it, and advanced from one struggle to another, till it succeeded. . . .

The fourth epoch has lasted from that time to our own days. It is chiefly marked in England by the progress of the representative system; on the Continent, by the development of the purely monarchical system, with which are associated local privileges, judicial institutions which exercise a powerful influence on political order, and some remnants of those assemblies which, in epochs anterior to the present, appeared under a more general form, but which now confine themselves to certain provinces, and are almost exclusively occupied with administrative functions. Under this system, though political liberty is no longer met with, barbarism and feudalism finally disappear before absolute power; interior order, the reconciliation of different classes, civil justice, public resources and information, make rapid progress;—nations become enlightened and prosperous, and their prosperity, material as well as moral, excites in them juster apprehensions of, and more earnest longings for, that representative system which they had sought in times when they possessed neither the knowledge nor the power requisite for its exercise and preservation.

This short epitome of facts has already indicated to you, gentlemen, the epochs towards which our studies will be principally directed. The objects of our search are the political instutions of various peoples. The representative system is that around which our researches will centre. . . . The second and the fourth epochs therefore, that is to say, feudalism and absolute power, will occupy us but little. We shall only speak of them so far as a consideration of them is necessary to connect and explain the periods which will more directly claim our attention. I purpose to study with you the first and the third epochs, and the fourth, so far as it relates to England. The first epoch, which shows us the German people establishing themselves on Roman soil—the struggle of their primitive institutions, or rather of their customs and habits, against the natural results of their new position,—in fine, the throes attending the earliest formation of modern nations,—has especial claims on our notice. I believe that, so far as regards political institutions, this time possessed nothing which deserves the name; but all the elements were there, in existence and commotion, as in the chaos which precedes creation. It is for us to watch this process, under which governments and peoples came into being. It is for us to ascertain whether, as has been asserted, public liberty and the representative system were actually there, whence some symptoms announced that they might one day emerge. When, in the third epoch, we see the feudal system being dissolved,—when we watch the first movements towards a representative government appear at the same time with the efforts of a central power which aims at becoming general and organized,—we shall recognize here, without difficulty, a subject which immediately belongs to us. We shall seek to learn what societies were then aroused, and by what means they have sought for trustworthy institutions, which might guarantee the continuance at once of order and of liberty. And when we have seen their hopes deceived by the calamities of the times, when we have detected in the vices of the social state, far more than in the influence of any disorderly or perverse desires, the causes of the ill-success of these magnanimous attempts, we shall be brought by our subject into the very midst of that people, then treated more leniently by fortune, which has paid dearly for free institutions, but which has guarded them to the last when they perished everywhere else, and which while preserving and developing them for itself, has offered to other nations, if not a model, yet certainly an example. . . .

Notes

1. I.e., England.—Ed.

Chapter 2 PARLIAMENT AN ASSEMBLY OF ESTATES ADMITTED TO POLITICAL POWER

WILLIAM STUBBS (1825-1901) was one of the more influential historians of the later nineteenth century. Making his reputation as an editor of texts, he was appointed Regius professor at Oxford University in 1866 and later served as bishop of Oxford. In his best known works he attributed the origin of Parliament in England to the political evolution of local communities and estates which were admitted by Edward I "to a share, a large share, in the process of government."

The idea of a constitution in which each class of society should, as soon as it was fitted for the trust, be admitted to a share of power and control, and in which national action should be determined by the balance maintained between the forces thus combined, never perhaps presented itself to the mind of any medieval politician. The shortness of life, and the jealousy inherent in and attendant on power, may account for this in the case of the practical statesman, although a long reign like that of Henry III might have given room for the experiment; and, whilst a strong feeling of jealousy subsisted throughout the middle ages between the king and the barons, there was no such strong feeling between the barons and the

From William Stubbs, *The Constitutional History of England* . . . , 3 vols. (Oxford: Clarendon, 1873-1878), II (4th ed.), 166-175 (abridged; footnotes omitted); *Select Charters and other illustrations of English Constitutional History* . . . , 8th ed. (Oxford: Clarendon, 1895), 35-36, 43-51 (abridged).

commons. But even the scholastic writers, amid their calculations of all possible combinations of principles in theology and morals, well aware of the difference between the 'rex politicus' who rules according to law and the tyrant who rules without it, and of the characteristics of monarchy, aristocracy and democracy, with their respective corruptions, contented themselves for the most part with balancing the spiritual and secular powers, and never broached the idea of a growth into political enfranchisement. Yet, in the long run, this has been the ideal towards which the healthy development of national life in Europe has constantly tended, only the steps towards it have not been taken to suit a preconceived theory. The immediate object in each case has been to draw forth the energy of the united people in some great emergency, to suit the convenience of party or the necessities of kings, to induce the newly admitted classes to give their money, to produce political contentment, or to involve all alike in the consciousness of common responsibility.

The history of the thirteenth century fully illustrates this. Notwithstanding the difference of circumstances and the variety of results, it is to this period that we must refer, in each country of Europe, the introduction, or the consolidation, for the first time since feudal principles had forced their way into the machinery of government, of national assemblies composed of properly arranged and organised Estates. The accepted dates in some instances fall outside the century. The first recorded appearance of town representatives in the Cortes of Aragon is placed in 1162; the first in Castille in 1169. The general courts of Frederick II in Sicily were framed in 1232: in Germany the cities appear by deputies in the diet of 1255, but they only begin to form a distinct part under Henry VII and Lewis of Bavaria; in France the States General are called together first in 1302. Although in each case the special occasions differ, the fact, that a similar expedient was tried in all, shows that the class to which recourse was for the first time had was in each country rising in the same or in a proportional degree, or that the classes which had hitherto monopolised power were in each country feeling the need of a reinforcement. The growth of the towns in wealth and strength, and the decline of properly feudal ideas in kings, clergy and barons, tended to the momentary parallelism. The way in which the crisis was met decided in each country the current of its history. In England the parliamentary system of the middle ages emerged from the policy of Henry II, Simon de Montfort and Edward I; in France the States General were so managed as to place the whole realm under royal absolutism; in Spain the long struggle ended in the sixteenth century in making the king despotic, but the failure of the constitution arose directly from the fault of its original structure. The Sicilian policy of Frederick passed away with his house. In Germany the disruption of all central government was reflected in the Diet; the national paralysis showed itself in a series of abortive attempts, few and far between, at united action, and the real life was diverted into provincial channels and dynastic designs.

The parliamentary constitution and England comprises, . . . not only a concentration of local machinery but an assembly of estates. The parliament of the present day, and still more clearly the parliament of Edward I, is a combination of these two theoretically distinct principles. The House of Commons now most distinctly represents the former idea, which is also conspicuous in the constitution of Convocation, and in that system of parliamentary representation of the clergy which was an integral part of Edward's scheme: it is to some extent seen in the present constitution of the House of Lords, in the case of the representative peers of Ireland and Scotland, who may also appeal for precedent to the same reign. It may be distinguished by the term local representation as distinct from class representation; for the two are not necessarily united, as our own history as well as that of foreign countries abundantly testifies. In some systems the local interest predominates over the class interest; in one the character of delegate eclipses the character of senator; in another all local character may disappear as soon as the threshold of the assembly is passed; in one there may be a direct connexion between the local representation and the rest of the local machinery; in another the central assembly may be constituted by means altogether different from those used for administrative purposes, and the representative system may be used as an expedient to supersede unmanageable local institutions; while, lastly, the members of the representative body may in one case draw their powers solely from their delegate or procuratorial character, and in another from that senatorial character which belongs to them as members of a council which possesses sovereignty or a share of it . . . the States General of France under Philip the Fair were a general assembly of clergy, barons, and town communities, in no way connected with any system of provincial estates, which indeed can hardly be said to have existed at the time. In Germany the representative elements of the Diet,—the prelates, counts and cities,—had a local arrangement and system of collective as distinct from independent voting; and in the general cortes of Aragon the provincial estates of Aragon, Catalonia and Valencia, were arranged in three distinct bodies in the same chamber. . . .

An assembly of Estates is an organised collection, made by representation or otherwise, of the several orders, states or conditions of men, who are recognised as possessing political power. A national council of clergy and barons is not an assembly of estates, because it does not include the body of the people, 'the plebs,' the simple freemen or commons, who on all constitutional theories have a right to be consulted as to their own taxation, if on nothing else. So long as the prelates and barons, the tenants-in-chief of the crown, met to grant an aid, whilst the towns and shires were consulted by special commissions, there was no meeting of estates. A county court, on the other hand, although it never bore in England the title of provincial estates, nor possessed the powers held by the provincial estates on the continent, was a really exhaustive assembly of this character.

The arrangement of the political factors in three estates is common, with some minor variations, to all the European constitutions, and depends on a principle of almost universal acceptance. . . . In France, both in the States General and in the provincial estates, the division is into 'gentz de l'eglise,' 'nobles,' and 'gentz des bonnes villes'. In England, after a transitional stage, in which the clergy, the greater and smaller barons, and the cities and boroughs, seemed likely to adopt the system used in Aragon and Scotland, and another in which the county and borough communities continued to assert an essential difference, the three estates of clergy, lords, and commons, finally emerge as the political constituents of the nation, or, in their parliamentary form, as the lords spiritual and temporal and the commons. This familiar formula in either shape bears the impress of history. The term 'commons' is not in itself an appropriate expression for the third estate; it does not signify primarily the simple freemen, the plebs, but the plebs organised and combined in corporate communities, in a particular way for particular purposes. The commons are the 'communitates' or 'universitates,' the organised bodies of freemen of the shires and towns; and the estate of the commons is the 'communitas communitatum,' the general body into which for the purposes of parliament those communities are combined. . . .

The long struggle of the constitution for existence ends with the reign of Edward I. This great monarch, whose commanding spirit, defining and organising power, and thorough honesty of character, place him in strong contrast not merely with his father, but with all the rest of our long line of kings, was not likely to surrender without a struggle the position which he had inherited. For more than twenty years he reigned as Henry II had done, showing proper respect for constitutional forms, but exercising the reality of despotic power. He loved his people, and therefore did not oppress them: they knew and loved him, and endured the pressure of taxation, which would not have been imposed if it had not been necessary. He admits them to a share, a large share, in the process of government: he develops and defines the constitution in its mechanical character in a way which Simon de Montfort had never contemplated. The organisation of parliament, of convocation, of the courts of law, of provincial jurisdiction, is elaborated and completed until it seems to be as perfect as it is at the present day; and the legislation is so full that the laws of the next three centuries are little more than a necessary expansion of it. But until he is compelled by the action of the barons, he retains the substance of royal power, the right to the purse-strings, the right to talliage the towns and the demesnes of the crown without a grant from the parliament. Edward I would not have been nearly so great a king as he was if he had not thought this right worth a struggle; nor if when that struggle was going against him, he had not seen that it was time to yield; nor if, when he had yielded, he had not determined honestly to abide by his concessions. The political party that forced him to the concession was not to be compared with the earlier combinations of the century: Bohun and Bigod had doubtless personal claims at heart, and not political ones: but they took advantage of a state of things which Edward saw could not be resisted. The confirmation of the Charters completes the present survey of political history.

The idea of constitutional government, defined by the measures of Edward I, and summed up in the legal meaning of the word parliament, implies four principles: first, the existence of a central or national assembly, a 'commune consilium regni;'[1] second, the representation in that assembly of all classes of the people, regularly summoned; third, the reality of the representation of the whole people, secured either by its presence in the council, or by the free election of the persons who are to represent it or any portion of it; and fourth, the assembly so summoned and elected must possess definite powers of taxation, legislation, and general political deliberation. . . .

Of the four normal powers of a national assembly, the judicial has never been exercised by the parliament as a parliament. The House of Commons is not, either by itself or in conjunction with the House of Lords, a court of justice: the House of Lords has inherited its jurisdiction from the Great Council. Another power, the political, or right of general deliberation on all national matters, is too vague in its extent to be capable of being chronologically defined; nor was it really vindicated by the parliament until a much later period than that on which we are now employed. The two most important remain, the legislative and the taxative, the tracing of whose history must complete our present survey.

1. The ancient theory that the laws were made by the king and witan co-ordinately, if it be an ancient theory, has within historic times been modified by the doctrine that the king enacted the laws with the counsel and consent of the witan. This is the most ancient form existing in enactments, and is common to the early laws of all the Teutonic races: it has of course always been still more modified in usage by the varying power of the king and his counsellors, and by the share that each was strong enough to vindicate in the process. Until the reign of John the varieties of practice may be traced chiefly in the form taken by the law on its enactment. The ancient laws are either drawn up as codes, like Alfred's, or as amendments of customs: often we have only the bare abstract of them, the substance that was orally transmitted from one generation of witan to another; where we have them in integrity the counsel and consent of the witan are specified. The laws of the Norman kings are put in the form of charters; the king in his sovereign capacity grants and confirms liberties and free customs to his people, but with the counsel and consent of his barons and faithful. Henry II issued most of his enactments as edicts or assizes, with a full rehearsal of the counsel and consent of his archbishops, bishops, abbots, priors, earls, barons, knights, and freeholders. The compact of John with the barons has the form of a charter, but, as already stated, is really a treaty based on articles proposed to him, and containing additional articles to secure execution. From the time of John the forms vary, and the reign of Henry III contains statutes of every shape—the charter, the assize, the articles proposed and accepted, and the special form of provisions, which are analogous to the canons of ecclesiastical councils. From the reign of Edward I the forms are those of statutes and ordinances, differing in some ascertained respects, the former formally

accepted in the parliament as laws of perpetual obligation, and enrolled: the latter proceeding from the king and his council rather than from the king and parliament, being more temporary in character, and not enrolled among the statutes. All alike express the counsel and consent with which the king fortifies his own enacting power: but several of the early statutes of Edward are worded as if that enacting power resided in the king and his ordinary council; and it is not clear whether this assumption is based on the doctrine of the scientific jurists who were addicted to the civil law, or on imitation of the practice of the French kings, just then made illustrious by the Establishments of Saint Lewis. . . .

Down to the end of the reign of Edward I it can hardly be said that the right of counsel was extended to the commons at all; it is in the next reign that their power of initiation by way of petition is first recognised. As late as the 18th of Edward I,[2] the statute Quia Emptores was passed by the king and barons, before the day for which the commons were summoned. As to the clergy, there is no doubt either that they exercised the right of petition or that the king occasionally made a statute at their request, with the counsel of the lords, and without reference to the commons; but acts so sanctioned were not regarded by the lawyers as of full authority, and are relegated, perhaps rightly, to the class of ordinances. Possibly the royal theory was that the right of petition belonged to both clergy and commons, whilst the counsel and consent of the lords only was indispensable. It was not until the 15th of Edward II that the voice of parliament, when revoking the acts of the ordainers, distinctly enunciated the principle that all matters to be established for the estate of the king and people 'shall be treated, accorded, and established in Parliaments by the king and by the assent of the prelates, earls, barons, and commonalty of the realm, according as it hath been hitherto accustomed'.[3]

2. The share of the commons in taxation takes precedence of their share in legislation. The power of voting money was more necessary than that of giving counsel. Of this power, as it existed up to the date of Magna Carta, enough has been said. The witenagemot, and its successor the royal council of barons, could impose the old national taxes; the ordinary feudal exactions were matters of common law and custom, and the amount of them was limited by usage. But the extraordinary aids which Henry II and his sons substituted for the Danegeld, and the taxes on the demesne lands of the crown, were arbitrary in amount and incidence; the former clearly requiring, and the latter, on all moral grounds, not less demanding, an act of consent on the part of the payers. This right was early recognised; even John, as we have seen, asked his barons sometimes for grants, and treated with the demesne lands and towns through the Exchequer, with the clergy through the bishops and archdeacons. Magna Carta enunciates the principle that the payers shall be called to the common council to vote the aids which had been previously negotiated separately;[4] but the clause was never confirmed by Henry III, nor was it applicable to the talliaging of demesne. It is as the towns begin to increase, and at the same time taxation ceases to be based solely on land and begins to affect personal as well

as real property, that the difficulties of the king and the hardships of the estates liable to talliage become important. The steps by which the king was compelled to give up the right of taking money without a parliamentary grant, are the same as those which led to the confirmation of the charters by Edward I. . . .

We have thus brought our sketch of Constitutional History to the point of time at which the nation may be regarded as reaching its full stature. It has not yet learned its strength, nor accustomed itself to economise its power. Its first vagaries are those of a people grown up, but not disciplined. To trace the process by which it learned the full strength of its organism—by which it learned to use its powers and forces with discrimination and effect—to act easily, effectually, and economically,—or, to use another metaphor, to trace the gradual wear of the various parts of the machinery, until all roughnesses were smoothed, and all that was superfluous, entangling, and confusing was got rid of, and the balance of forces adjusted, and action made manageable and intelligible, and the power of adaptation to change of circumstances fully realised,—is the story of later politics, of a process that is still going on, and must go on as the age advances, and men are educated into wider views of government, national unity, and political responsibility. We stop, however, with Edward I, because the machinery is now completed, the people are at full growth. The system is raw and untrained and awkward, but it is complete. The attaining of this point is to be attributed to the defining genius, the political wisdom, and the honesty of Edward I, building on the immemorial foundation of national custom; fitting together all that Henry I had planned, Henry II organised, and the heroes of the thirteenth century had inspired with fresh life and energy.

Notes

1. "Common council of the realm;" cf. *Magna Carta*, p. 144.—Ed.
2. 1290.—Ed.
3. I.e., the Statute of York (1322).—Ed.
4. See p. 144.

Part Two

PARLIAMENT IN ENGLAND

Chapter 3 PARLIAMENT A SESSION OF THE KING'S COUNCIL FOR BROADLY JUDICIAL BUSINESS

After Stubbs, F. W. MAITLAND
(1850-1906), appointed Downing professor
at Cambridge University in 1888, was the
scholar who most significantly interpreted
the early history of parliament. His work as
editor of legal texts and as historian of
English law is distinguished by prodigious
erudition, incisive analysis, and inimitable
grace. Despite his own disclaimer, his
conception of Parliament as basically a
meeting of the king's councillors was a major
revision of enduring influence on scholarship.

On the 12th of November 1304 King Edward issued from Burstwick writs for a
parliament to be holden at Westminster on the 16th of February 1305. He was on
his way back from Scotland. He kept Christmas at Lincoln and was there as late as
the 12th of January. On the 22nd he was at Spalding and thence he issued a second
set of writs. Events, he said, had happened which made it impossible for him to be
at Westminster on the appointed day, so the parliament was postponed to the 28th
of February. Slowly and by a circuitous route he travelled southward, for we hear
of him at Walsingham, Swaffham, Thetford, Bury St. Edmunds, Exning, Wilbraham,
Royston, Braughing, Standon, Wades Hill, Ware, Waltham. On the 26th of January
he addressed a letter under his privy seal to the chancellor, which may perhaps
explain the postponement. He expected that in the ensuing parliament the clergy

From F. W. Maitland, *Records of the Parliament holden at Westminster*... (A. D. 1305)
(London: Rolls Series, 1893), pp. xxxiv-xxxvi, lxxxvi-lxxxix (abridged; footnotes omitted).

would call him in question and he directed that a search should be made in the chancery for any documents which might bear upon the matters in dispute. By other letters under the privy seal dated on the 5th of February, of which we must speak at greater length hereafter, he directed the appointment of receivers and auditors of petitions; he desired that the petitions should, so far as was possible, be disposed of before his arrival at Westminster. Meanwhile the sheriffs of Kent, Surrey and Sussex had been bidden to send up great quantities of corn and ale to Westminster for the maintenance of the king's household. On the 27th he entered London and stayed at the Hospital of St. Katharine near the Tower. On the 28th the parliament was opened at Westminster.

It was a full parliament in our sense of that term. The three estates of the realm met the king and his council. The great precedent of 1295 had been followed and, if the writs of summons were punctually obeyed, the assembly was a large one. By rights there should have been present some ninety-five prelates, about a hundred and forty-five representatives of the inferior clergy, nine earls (if we include the Prince of Wales and the Earl of Angus), ninety-four barons, seventy-four knights of the shires, and about two hundred citizens and burgesses; altogether some six hundred men.[1] Besides these we must take account of thirty-three members of the king's council to whom writs were sent, and, as we shall see hereafter, there were yet other men present and performing important duties, men who had a special knowledge of Scotland and Gascony.

This assembly was kept together for just three weeks. On the 21st of March a proclamation was made telling the archbishops, bishops and other prelates, earls, barons, knights, citizens and burgesses in general that they might go home, but must be ready to appear again if the king summoned them. Those bishops, earls, barons, justices and others who were members of the council were to remain behind and so were all those who had still any business to transact. But the 'parliament' was not at an end. Many of its doings that are recorded on our roll were done after the estates had been sent home. The king remained at Westminster, surrounded by his councillors, and his parliament was still in session as a 'full' and 'general' parliament as late as the 5th and 6th of April. Easter day fell on the 18th of that month, and its approach seems to have put an end to the prolonged session. Early in May the king began a tour through the home counties. He proposed to hold another 'parliament,' which however, so far as we know, was not to be an assembly of the estates, on the 15th of July, but this he postponed first to the 15th of August and then to the 15th of September.

Now if we are to frame any exact conception of the body or various bodies of men by whom the business that is recorded on our roll was transacted, and of the mode in which they dealt with that business, it seems necessary that we should understand the composition of the king's council. Unfortunately, as is well known, the council of Edward I is still for us an ill-defined group of men. Writs of summons and writs for wages will often teach us the names of all the barons who were called to a parliament and enable us to know who it was that represented the pettiest boroughs, and yet we cannot enumerate with any certainty the members of the council. . . . We are dealing with Edward I, the wise and vigorous king. Under his hand institutions which to our eyes seem to have in them many flaws, flaws which may easily become yawning clefts, are doing their appointed work without much friction. We can hardly look back to his time through the fourteenth century without imagining that there must be some jealous dislike of the council, an aristocratic jealousy on the part of the nobles, a professional jealousy on the part of the judges and common lawyers. But do we really see this? If not, then our problem as to the constitution of the supreme tribunal becomes simpler. It may be further simplified if we try to make it a concrete problem. Indubitably this supreme tribunal is the council. The question whether it is also the house of lords may be divided into two. First, we ought to ask whether every prelate and baron had a right to sit in the council though he had not been invited to do so. Secondly, we ought to ask whether those members of the council who were neither prelates nor barons were fully competent members of the tribunal.

To neither of these questions must we here give a dogmatic answer, but in connexion with the first it may be right that we should ask a yet further question, namely, whether we are not introducing an inappropriate idea and burdening ourselves with an unnecessary anachronism when we talk of any man having a right to sit in this or any other court of law? We must put duty in the first line, right in the second. We have learnt to do this when discussing the constitution of those county courts which send knights to the house of commons; must we not also do it when we are discussing the constitution of the house of lords and of the council? In 1305 the baron, who had come from Yorkshire or Devonshire, had been compelled to spend three weeks in London at his own cost, for he was paid no wages. Did he very much want to spend another three weeks there hearing dreary petitions concerning the woes of Scots and Gascons? At a later time a desire for political power and for social pre-eminence will make the English baron eager to insist on his right to a writ of summons, eager to take a part, however subordinate, in all that is done by the house of lords. But in Edward I's day the baronage is hardly as yet a well-defined body, and it may be that there are many men who, unable to foresee that their 'blood' is being 'ennobled' for ever and ever, are not best pleased when they receive a writ which tells them that, leaving their homes and affairs, they must journey and labour in the king's service, and all this at their own cost. Thus for many years one great constitutional question can remain in suspense. It is not raised, no one wishes to raise it. So long as the king does not impose taxes or issue statutes without the consent of the baronage, the baron hopes that the king will mind his own business (and it is his business to govern the realm) and allow other folk to mind theirs.

Of the second of our two questions but one word can here be said. If we fix our gaze on the council which remains in constant session and 'in full parliament' at

Westminster for several weeks after the generality of prelates and barons have departed, we shall have some difficulty in believing that those councillors who are neither prelates nor barons are taking but a subordinate part in the work that is done; for example, that when the council is sitting as a judicial tribunal, the opinions of the two chief justices, Brabazon and Hengham, are of less importance than the opinions of two barons who are no lawyers. Once more let us remember that until very lately the jurisdiction of the king's council has been regarded as being substantially the same thing as the jurisdiction of that court over which Brabazon presides.

Perhaps more than enough has already been said about these controverted matters; but it seemed necessary to remind readers, who are conversant with the 'parliaments' of later days, that about the parliaments of Edward I's time there is still much to be discovered, and that should they come to the opinion that a session of the king's council is the core and essence of every *parliamentum*, that the documents usually called 'parliamentary petitions' are petitions to the king and his council, that the auditors of petitions are committees of the council, that the rolls of parliament are the records of the business done by the council,—sometimes with, but much more often without, the concurrence of the estates of the realm,—that the highest tribunal in England is not a general assembly of barons and prelates, but the king's council, they will not be departing very far from the path marked out by books that are already classical.

Notes

1. For writs of summons in 1295, see p. 147 (J); for a comparison of size, see the summons to the Catalan *Cort* of 1333, p. 149 (M).—Ed.

Chapter 4 REPRESENTATION AS OBLIGATORY SERVICE AT THE KING'S COMMAND

Nineteenth-century liberal scholarship had easily assumed that representation in medieval parliaments arose as a welcome concession to aspiring knights and townsmen. DÉSIRÉ PASQUET (1870-1928), a French specialist in English and American history, was not the first to contest this view; his achievement was to argue cogently that the original deputies were strengthening rather than limiting the king's power, their attendance being more in the nature of an administrative obligation than a constitutional right.

Our investigation has shown us that the convening of representatives of the counties and towns in parliament was essentially the work of the crown. This convening is to be traced to remote origins. The custom of summoning four knights, on behalf of the county, before the king's court appeared to us to have been firmly established in the reign of Richard I. And parliament is only an amplified form of the king's court. In the thirteenth century the kings gradually adopted the custom of summoning several counties at once, and even all the counties of England together. Through the sheriffs they summoned before themselves and their council two, three or four discreet knights to represent a county and to speak in its name. Sometimes, when the circumstances seemed to demand it, they particularly ordered that these

From Désiré Pasquet, *An Essay on the Origins of the House of Commons*, tr. R. G. D. Laffan (Cambridge, Eng., 1925), pp. 223-230 (abridged). Reprinted by permission of Cambridge University Press.

knights should be elected by the county court. On other occasions the sheriffs were merely commanded to provide for the attendance of four knights, as in the case of an ordinary judicial citation. The purpose of the summons was not always the same. The knights might be required to give evidence in an inquest on the administration of the sheriffs. Or their assent might be required for an aid, the collection of which would be difficult without their co-operation. Lastly, in its struggles against the magnates, the crown was not above seeking the help of the numerous and powerful class of gentry, who held a large portion of the land of England and in the county courts administered the countryside.

At a moment of crisis, when nearly all the magnates were opposed to him, Simon de Montfort, then ruling in the king's name, summoned to parliament not only representatives of the county communities, but also representatives of the town communities.[1]

For the counties and towns, as for the prelates and barons, the summons was in the nature of a feudal obligation. Attendance at the king's parliament was not a right, but a duty or, to adopt the contemporary expression, a service—the service, or suit, of court. As regards the knights and burgesses, the compulsory character of the summons is very clearly shown by the practice of demanding security for their appearance; a practice which was in use from the beginning of Edward I's reign and does not seem to have been then an innovation. We never find the counties and towns claiming to be summoned to parliament as of right. The knights and burgesses were by no means anxious to repair to London, York or Shrewsbury in order to waste valuable time over the king's business and to play a part of but small importance in the king's assembly. Even if the knights, long accustomed to such summons, discharged their service without much grumbling, the towns offered a passive resistance which in the end often defeated the perseverance of the sheriffs and the wishes of the king.

The formation of the house of commons has long been represented as the last step in a development which began with the Great Charter, was continued by the Provisions of Oxford and the great parliament of 1265, and ended in the "model" parliament of 1295. This development was held to have been caused by the alliance of the magnates, gentry and bourgeoisie, who all united to oppose the excessive power of the crown and succeeded in limiting the royal authority. But the study of the documents has led us to quite other conclusions. The nation did not demand representation in the king's parliament. It was the king who imposed on his subjects the duty of sending him their representatives.

Edward I changed an occasional expedient into a regular custom, not in order to associate the whole nation with himself in the work of government, but in order to strengthen the royal power. He only summoned the representatives of the commons when such a course seemed to him to serve his own interests; and often the most important agenda were discussed in their absence. If in the end he made a practice of summoning them almost regularly, this was because he perceived that the previous consent of the knights and burgesses greatly facilitated the collection of aids and even enabled the government to collect rather more than would otherwise have been possible. Another reason was that the petitions, in which the delegates of the communities begged him to redress wrongs irremediable by the ordinary processes of the law, gave him full information on the condition of his kingdom and enabled him to make all aware of the strength of the royal arm. Every abuse of power by a great lord, every injustice by a servant of the crown, every invasion of the royal rights was denounced before the king's court; and thus the sessions of the full parliaments carried on the grand inquests of the beginning of the reign. Lastly, the assemblies of representatives from counties and towns embodied one of the fundamental ideas of Edward's policy. In parliament, as formed by him, the old feudal distinction between tenants-in-chief and sub-vassals was entirely abolished. The king had before him only subjects. Despite its feudal form, the summoning of the commons was an essentially anti-feudal measure, the object of which was to strengthen the central power and to subject all the inhabitants of the realm, of whatever rank in the feudal hierarchy, to the direct authority of the monarch. In this respect Edward continued the policy of Henry II and emulated Philippe le Bel.

But Edward's plans did not succeed; or rather they succeeded only in part. The assembly of representatives from counties and towns did indeed rapidly achieve the destruction of the feudal system of society. But it did not result in an increase of the royal power, as Edward had hoped.

About the middle of the fourteenth century the house of commons, which existed only in embryo in the model parliaments of Edward I, assumed the character of an established and clearly defined institution. We may ask why the knights associated themselves with the burgesses. Between these two groups, which were elected by the communities of the realm and represented the "poor folk of the land" and whose constituents paid the greater part of the royal taxes, was there any natural affinity drawing them together? Or were the knights excluded from the baronage by the growing tendency towards the constitution of an hereditary peerage? It is difficult to say. Anyhow, in the early years of Edward III's reign, we clearly see the two groups of representatives drawing together. It is uncertain whether the knights and burgesses united in one body at the parliaments of March and September 1332. It is almost certain that they did so at the parliaments of December 1332 and January 1333. Undeniably they did so in 1339 and 1341. At first the co-operation between the two elements, of which the new institution was formed, was not perfect. The bourgeoisie were an inferior class, subject to heavier charges than was the community of the realm. Sometimes the royal government still negotiated separately with them, as before. But the distinction between the knights and burgesses gradually became a mere question of their respective degrees of influence in parliament.

Parliament long retained the appearance of a single whole. As councillors of the king, the lords remained in the great hall of the council. They did not form a separate chamber; and the term "house of lords" does not appear till the sixteenth century. Even the deputies of the commons, although they established themselves in the chapter-house of Westminster Abbey and there deliberated apart, formed a committee of parliament . . . rather than a real "house." From time to time they crossed the road to appear "in parliament," their speaker at their head. It was only very slowly that the original unity of parliament ceased to have any real existence and was reduced to a mere form; and even more slowly did the commons come at last to play a decisive part in the English constitution.

But the amalgamation of the knights and burgesses in the house of commons is one of the facts that have determined the development of that constitution. Without the knights the house of commons would have formed a very feeble third estate, and would have cut a sorry figure beside the king and the haughty and turbulent aristocracy that arose from the ruins of the old feudalism. But the nobility and the crown had to reckon with the knights, whose wealth, legal knowledge and influence in the counties rendered them formidable alike to the royal officers and to the liveried swashbucklers of the great lords.

Another fact which had a decisive effect on the development of English institutions was the secession of the clergy, who, as an order, gradually ceased to attend parliament and retired to their convocations, just at the time when the house of commons was being formed. As has often been observed, the secession of the clergy destroyed that system of three estates, which would have rendered difficult the development of parliamentary institutions. The lords and the commons alone remained to face the king.

The lords and the commons were not always allied. Nor, on the other hand, did the commons always support the king's government, as Edward I had hoped, and as they did during part of Richard II's reign. Between the nobility and the king they more than once played the part of arbiters, sometimes without glory, but not always without profit. They also took advantage of the king's continual need of money, arising from the great campaigns and glorious victories in France. Still using the formulae of an extreme humility, they forced the kings to grant their petitions by only consenting to aids on certain conditions or at the end of the parliamentary session. Very slowly, by a series of precedents, they established their supremacy in financial matters and circumscribed that royal prerogative, which had previously been almost unlimited.

At the end of the fifteenth century, when the nobility had been destroyed and the monarchy seemed to have become all-powerful, in reality it was too late for the establishment of absolute power in England. The old forms, consecrated by two centuries of practice, survived the despotism of the Tudors; and in the seventeenth century the instrument, which Edward I had intended to make one of the weapons of the royal authority, was turned against the king.

Note

1. In 1264; the writ may be read p. 145.—Ed.

Chapter 5 PARLIAMENT AS SUCH A DISTINCTIVE AND RECOGNIZED COURT OF JUSTICE

H. G. RICHARDSON (b. 1884) and G. O. SAYLES (b. 1901) have long collaborated on the institutional history of medieval England. Rigorous, iconoclastic, finding little to satisfy them in prevailing interpretations, they have undertaken to re-examine almost every major problem in a vast field; their *Governance of Mediaeval England from the Conquest to Magna Carta* (1963) is to have a sequel. What follows, taken from a summary refutation of their critics, is their argument, perpetuating Maitland's doctrine in a refined form, that Parliament, so-called, was a recognized form of court without necessarily having political functions or representative attendance.

In 1258 the committee of Twenty-Four, appointed to reform the realm, determined that there should be three parliaments a year, and they proceeded to prescribe the proper constitution of a parliament or, rather, the minimum baronial representation there. It is clear from contemporary documents that the council minute which records the decision taken on this matter leaves much unsaid. While the Provisions of Oxford speak of the "elected councillors" (meaning the Fifteen) and of the representation of the *commune* (of barons) by twelve of their number, a parliament was understood to include a substantial ministerial element (without which it could not function) and could expand to a much more numerous assembly than the prescriptions of the Twenty-Four might suggest. Again, we are told no

From H. G. Richardson and G. O. Sayles, *Parliaments and Great Councils in Medieval England* (London: Stevens and Sons, 1961), pp. 1-3, 5-12, 15-16, 43-45, 49 (abridged; footnotes omitted). Reprinted by permission of Stevens and Sons.

more of the business to be transacted in parliament than that the king's "elected councillors" should be present "to survey the state of the realm and to discuss the common interests of the king and the kingdom." Indeed, if all we had to go upon was this minute, our conception of the English parliament under Henry III would be very vague. Writing in 1260, the king had, however, occasion to be a little more precise: justice was administered in parliament to all and sundry and, with the king's consent, there might be a change [in the law] or a new ordinance. And then, towards the close of the century, the author of *Fleta* described parliament in a way that might be taken as an elaboration of Henry's words. "In his parliaments the king in council holds his court.... There judicial doubts are determined, new remedies are devised for wrongs newly brought to light, and justice is dispensed to everyone according to his deserts." In their different ways the three documents appear to be describing an easily recognisable institution, a court set apart from, and set over, other courts. Indeed, if this were not the case, it is difficult to understand how, a few years before *Fleta* was written, there could have been dispatched from Ireland to England a treasury clerk, Alexander of London, whose duty it was to be present at three parliaments (which seem to be readily identifiable) and there to prosecute and defend the king's interests.

We could add, and we have indeed cited elsewhere, some scores of examples from the thirteenth century which seem to show that men understood exactly what a parliament was and knew precisely where and when parliaments were held. And in the belief that the many entries in official records had a meaning for contemporaries, we have gone so far as to construct tables showing the incidence of English Parliaments and we have even ventured to tabulate Scottish and Irish parliaments. We have also accepted, and even added to, the list of French parliaments constructed by other scholars. Nay more, we have edited two substantial volumes of parliamentary records and ascribed them, we believed correctly, to identifiable parliaments. But now, we are assured, all this work was beating the air, our categories and classifications mere fantasies begotten of illusion. When clerks in the chancery, the exchequer, the courts of justice, were to all appearance summoning and adjourning to parliament, recording solemn acts in parliament, they knew not the significance of what they did. We must picture the clerk Alexander dispatched from Ireland to seek, not once but three times, an *ignis fatuus*, a vague uncertain assembly, that might be called a parliament or treaty or colloquy or council, which, by some marvellous stroke of good fortune, he not only found but in which he performed the business he was required to undertake: and then, to crown all, he managed to obtain payment for the services he had rendered. A veritable *conte de fée....*[1]

The assumption that "parliament" is a vague, uncertain conception, a word used haphazardly by medieval clerks, is nothing new. "Parliament," said A. F. Pollard, "is *vox et preterea nihil*: there is nothing to distinguish it from other assemblies called in pursuance of the 14th article of Magna Carta requiring the special and general summons of tenants-in-chief to give consent to extraordinary feudal aids." But this statement he justified only by a reference to the chronicles excerpted by Stubbs in the *Select Charters* and by a somewhat confused appeal to the more easily accessible records of Edward I's parliaments. Seemingly Pollard, like many others, was misled by the distinction Stubbs had drawn between "the terminal session of the select council, the session of the great council, and the session of the commune concilium of the three estates," to all of which "the name of parliament, the king's parliament, belonged." "In the Rolls of Parliament," he added, "the confusion of name and distinction of function are still more conspicuous, for most of the early documents preserved under that name belong to the sessions of the council for judicial business . . . ." Stubbs did not argue his case. He did not invent it. He borrowed it, without acknowledgment, from the Reports of the Lords Committees on the Dignity of a Peer. Pollard was too acute to be misled by this pretence of learning. He saw, for example, the hollowness of the conception of "the three estates." But he lacked the leisure or the patience to assemble and assimilate the material for the early history of the English parliament: he was no medievalist. He seems to have been on the verge of accepting the "regular sessions" of the records as the true parliaments, scouting the idea that there could be anything vague and uncertain about a scheme which involved adjournments from one parliament to the next parliament. But the tradition of "the two kinds of meetings," still held by medievalists despite the evidence, was too strong: it remained to befog him and not only him, but his readers and his critics.

Now let us repeat what we said long ago, supported by a plenitude of evidence, "that parliaments are of one kind only and that, when we have stripped every non-essential away, the essence of them is the dispensing of justice by the king or by someone who in a very special sense represents the king." To these words and their implication, which have caused difficulty—unnecessary difficulty perhaps—we shall return. Let us say here that they are plainly contrary to all that Stubbs implied when, borrowing, as was his wont, an error of the Lords Committees, he spoke of a "model parliament" in 1295; they are plainly contrary to what countless teachers, uncritically reproducing Stubbs, have proceeded to teach their pupils. The primary criterion by which an assembly is to be assessed is, we assert, that of function and not the presence or absence from the king's court of particular persons or some particular class of suitor. This criterion we believe to have been the contemporary criterion: function determined whether or not a particular session of the king's council was parliament and was so termed. The doctrine advanced by Stubbs, that the presence or absence of the "three estates," in particular of representatives of the counties and shires, is a valid criterion by which to determine whether or not an assembly was a parliament, is sheer anachronism: in the face of contemporary evidence to the contrary it is an absurdity. It is clear that under Edward I and Edward II there was no convention whereby the representatives of either shires or boroughs were necessarily summoned to parliament and, as Stubbs himself was constrained to admit, there was no restriction of the name of parliament to assemblies in which they were present. To apply such a test even to the parliaments of Edward III would be highly questionable. We have but to turn to the history of parliament in Ireland at this period to learn that not until towards the end of his reign was it beginning to be thought essential to ensure the presence of representatives of shires and boroughs. Even were we to admit the existence of a recognised convention whereby shires and boroughs were represented in the English parliaments of Edward III, we could not then argue, as Mr. Plucknett does, that where the commons are there also is parliament. This is to fall into an obvious logical fallacy. Again, it is patently false to assert, as Stubbs asserted, that "the representation of all classes of the people is necessary for the complete organisation of a national council"—whatever that may mean—"and that complete organisation is legally constituted by summons to parliament." He is thinking of his "model" of 1295. Yet after that year the author of *Fleta* knew only that in the king's parliaments there were present prelates, barons and others learned in the law. Of any further elements he said nothing; of national councils he said nothing; indeed, to speak as Stubbs speaks is to use not the language of the Middle Ages but the tendentious jargon of the political theorists of his own time. If we prefer *Fleta* to Stubbs, it is because we prefer truth to fiction, plain history to baseless theory.

Like every judicial and administrative tribunal—and it is only gradually that the distinction between them becomes clear as the Middle Ages advance—parliament evolves and changes. What may be said of it in the thirteenth century will not be true of it in the fifteenth: the parliament of *Fleta* is not the parliament of Fortescue. And since parliament was not the creation of a legislative act nor, so far as we can tell, a conscious creation at all, we cannot give a date to its inception. Bracton, conservative that he was, never uses the word parliament. He knows of an afforced court where the community of the realm and the baronage are present, but he gives that court no specific name. We can hardly be wrong, however, in equating Bracton's *universitas regni et baronagium*[2] with the *commune* of the Provisions of Oxford, who were to elect twelve representatives to meet the king and his council in parliament. But it is not every meeting between the council and the Twelve that constitutes a parliament. Since the position seems still to be misunderstood, let us explain what the arrangements were. It would have been clearly impracticable for the Fifteen, "cunseilers le rei esluz," to be in constant attendance as a body upon the king, and in the Michaelmas parliament of 1259 the relation of the Fifteen to the small body of councillors attendant on the king was clarified. The Fifteen were to be represented by two or three of their number: these were to be *"mesne gent,"* that is of middling status, words which exclude bishops and earls. Their invidious task was to decide whether any weighty affair (*grant bossoine*) that might arise could be decided by their advice or could be deferred until the next terminal parliament or, if it could not be delayed, justified summoning by writ the whole of the Fifteen. Now it seems clear from the terms of the chancellor's oath that a weighty affair meant, at least normally, the grant by the king of wardships, money or escheats of any considerable amount, for such grants could not be made without the assent of the "great council" or the majority of them. It seems also clear that these afforced meetings would not be specially summoned parliaments but afforced councils, for which provision had been made at Oxford, to which both the Fifteen and also the Twelve might be summoned. Here, then, we have assemblies of the same composition, some of which, those meeting at fixed terms, are parliaments, while others, meeting occasionally and not periodically, are not parliaments. We see that the insurgent barons have seized upon the word "parliament," a popular word and hardly yet a word of court, and have applied it to one kind of afforced council. In doing so they have given "parliament" a technical meaning, for periodicity implies definition: there cannot be a periodical occurrence of something that is not defined. What the technical meaning of parliament was we shall examine in the light of such evidence as is available; but we may say, in advance, that there seems no reason to suppose that Henry III's parliaments differed in character from those of Edward I nor that their distinguishing characteristic was not the dispensing of justice....

We trust that we have made two things clear: that from the time parliamentary history becomes recognisable and continuous, a parliament in England is an afforced session of the king's council, and that there may be other afforced sessions of the king's council, indistinguishable in constitution, which are not parliaments. To say this is not to say that at these other sessions there might not be performed any, or perhaps all, of the functions performed in parliament. If we were to assert that this was not possible, we should be asserting that there was some limitation upon the powers of the king in council.... But to say that there is no limitation upon the powers of the king in council is not to say that these powers will be exercised without regard to the conventions of the time. It is clear that already in 1258 a parliament has an authority, a status, superior to that of other afforced sessions of the council, and it would appear to be a corollary, for which there is much evidence, that in parliament specially solemn acts may be expected to be performed, a higher justice administered....

The work of the Ordainers[3] was perhaps inept; but at least they were speaking of things they understood and among those things was parliament. They may not have viewed parliament in precisely the same light as the reformers of 1258, yet what they said of it shows that they had in mind the same institution, though this institution had evolved in half a century. Parliament to them was a quite distinctive institution: there was nothing in the least vague about it. That anyone could read the Ordinances and come to a contrary opinion might seem incredible, had it not happened. Moreover, when we compare these contemporary descriptions of parliamentary business with the fairly voluminous records that have survived from the reigns of Edward I and Edward II, we perceive that there is absolute congruity. Parliament, or, rather, the king in council in parliament, is doing exactly those things that *Fleta* and the Ordinances would lead us to expect.

It is against this background that the parliaments of Edward III must be regarded. The feature which distinguishes the parliaments of Edward III from those of his predecessors is the invariable presence of representatives of the commons and the development of the common petition. In the course of the fourteenth century this development greatly influenced parliamentary procedure. It gave a new form to legislation, which tended increasingly to be based, at least notionally, upon a petition presented by the commons, and it largely drove the private petitioner from parliament to seek his remedy elsewhere. That these changes were deliberately devised by the revolutionary government of 1327 it is impossible to believe. The change in legislative procedure derived from the enhanced status of the baronage, the origin of whose right, as peers, to sit as judges in parliament can be traced to their contest with Edward II. Judges, however, cannot at the same time be petitioners, and petitions of general import fell to be presented by the representatives of the commons, if they were to be presented at all. It was once fashionable to believe that the presence of the commons in parliament was secured by the Statute of York of 1322: we need waste no words on this mischievous doctrine, without warrant in contemporary documents, which abundantly disclose the origin and purpose of the statute. The commons were present in the revolutionary parliament of 1327 because it was politically convenient to have them there. They continued to be summoned for the same reason. They had, in fact, been increasingly summoned under Edward II and, after years of uninterrupted summons under Edward III, habit hardened into right. But we can point to no formal legislative act that required their presence or prescribed their characteristic function in the new reign, while the changes in petitory procedure were too gradual to permit us to believe that these were deliberately contrived. To assume that the presence or absence of the commons can be taken as a test of the nature of the assemblies called in the early years of Edward III introduces a rule of law for which there is no evidence. It is, as we have said, a logical fallacy to go further and assume that, where the commons are, there also is parliament. . . .

As, we believe, we were the first to demonstrate, business in great variety came before parliament in its earlier years. Nor would there seem to be any reason why any matter that might come before the king's council should not come before the king in council in parliament, if this were a suitable occasion. We have at no time suggested that, because the distinctive quality of parliament was the dispensing of justice, this was its sole purpose, though we have emphasised, and rightly emphasised, the unique importance of this function in face of the denial by Stubbs that parliament, in the true sense, as he conceived it, had such a function at all. If his doctrine—the doctrine that parliament is a "national council," "the concentration of the three estates"—had been historically valid, then the king's council, which dispensed justice, would have stood outside parliament, and Maitland's suggestion (for he professed to go no further) that "a session of the king's council is the core and essence of every *parliamentum*" would have been absurd. In truth, it is Stubbs's doctrine that is unwarrantable, and no one would venture to defend it; but there is still, it would seem, great reluctance to abandon the inferences that proceeded from it. The imaginary parliament of Stubbs, or something very like it, has been denominated the "representative parliament" in contradistinction to the "pre-representative parliament," and we have been presented afresh with a picture, made familiar in another guise by Stubbs and Pollard, of a plurality of parliaments. The dichotomy seems, in any case, to be false, since it suggests that there was a point of time at which "pre-representative parliaments" ceased and "representative parliaments" began. If, however, we take our starting point in 1258 and continue to 1327, we find that, over a period little short of seventy years, parliaments to which representatives of shires or towns were summoned, for one purpose or another, alternated with parliaments to which there was no such summons. Parliaments of the latter type predominated, it is true, until the year 1300 and parliaments of the former type thereafter; but there is no "pre" or "post." "Pre-representative" and "representative" parliaments co-existed. There were not two kinds of parliament, though in some there was business for which it was deemed desirable to summon representatives of the "commons"; but, as Pollard said, "they probably took a less active part in parliament than the audience does in a public meeting of today."

The true dividing line is 1327. From 1327 onwards all parliaments included representatives of the shires and boroughs. The intention behind this development was doubtless political, but, as we have explained, a significant change had taken place. The emergence of the doctrine of peerage meant that the barons could no longer be petitioners, no longer speak as the mouthpiece of the *commune*. In 1306 the knights of the shire could form one body with the barons. In 1327, although they are still quite distinct from the burgesses, the knights act in common with them: a step has been taken which will in process of time give parliament a house of commons. During the reign of Edward II there had been wrought, unwittingly and without foresight, a great constitutional change. The significance of this change may not at first have been appreciated, but before long Bishop Granson of Exeter could put the position in a striking metaphor. "By its nature the substance of the Crown lies primarily in the king's person, as head, and in the peers of the land, as members . . . and in this way the Crown is so conditioned that there cannot be severance without dividing the kingship." As was said a century or so later, "the king is intrinsicate within his council." If, on the other hand, the doctrine of peerage was significant in giving the representatives of shires and boroughs a constant and continuous function in parliament, that of presenting common petitions, it was equally significant in giving a constitution to the council, whether in parliament or out of parliament. There was, however, no sudden or marked breach with the past. Bishops, earls and barons had hitherto been present in the council with judges and ministers; but henceforward the status, as well as the number, of the king's servants in the council was to decline while the status of the peers was to be exalted.

Though the constitution of the council might change, its dominance in parliament was undiminished. . . .

We have been an unconscionable time making an end, but since last we wrote of the English parliament many things have been said which invited comment. Let these be our last words. The discussion of the nature and characteristics of parliament under Henry III and the first three Edwards threatens to become a vain dispute about the niceties of language. In such disputes we have no interest. Our concern is with historical realities, with what was done and said in the thirteenth and fourteenth centuries. So long as these are described in sufficient fullness and with sufficient accuracy, it matters little what terms are used, provided the terms are reasonably unambiguous and fitting to the century to which they are applied. But we confess that, just as we deprecate the selection of evidence to support some preconceived conclusion, so we wince at such phrases as "political assembly" or "representative parliament," which have a meaning at the present day that is not apposite to the reigns of Henry III and the first two Edwards, not even to those few parliaments where "politics" may be discerned in the clashes between the king and a baronial opposition. "In his parliaments the king in council holds his court in the presence of prelates, earls, barons, nobles and others learned in the law." What have "politics," what has "representation," to do with these parliaments?

Notes

1. Here the authors cite recent scholars who doubt whether "parliament" had a precise meaning to medieval people.—Ed.
2. "University" [i.e., "community"] of the realm and the baronage."—Ed.
3. An executive council for administrative reform imposed on Edward II in 1311.—Ed.

Chapter 6 PARLIAMENT BASICALLY A POLITICAL AND DELIBERATIVE BODY

While Richardson and Sayles represent the extreme reaction against Stubbs, BERTIE WILKINSON (b. 1898), emeritus professor of medieval history at the University of Toronto, has effectively revived the interpretation of the original Parliament as a political assembly. Wilkinson's discussion, here excerpted from his major work, is characteristically lucid, sensible and careful; it should be read for its differences from older views of parliament as well as its resemblance to them.

... The first step towards a true understanding of both parliament and council is to retrace the step which Maitland took with such scholarly reserve and caution in 1893, and to give back to both a separate identity and distinctive position and functions in the state. However we regard parliament, we must cease to regard it, on the evidence so far examined, as a mere expansion of the council; and its functions are not to be confused with those of the king. Parliament did not contain the council in the sense that the actions of the one were merely an extension of those of the other; many of the things which were done in parliament were not done by parliament. We must seek to find the essence of parliament not in what was done within, or by part of the assembly, but in what was done by the whole. We must, it

From Bertie Wilkinson, *Studies in the Constitutional History of the Thirteenth and Fourteenth Centuries*, 2d ed. (Manchester University Press, 1952), pp. 14-29, 50-51, 54 (abridged; footnotes, titles omitted). Reprinted by permission of the author and of Manchester University Press.

seems probable, revert to the older idea of a full parliament as an assembly in which contemporaries could see reflected not the king's council but, in some sense, the *universitas regni,* the assembled power and majesty of the realm. It was something bigger in every sense than a gathering of the king's personal advisers. It is there if anywhere, we may conclude, that we shall discover what the essence of the medieval parliament was.

If parliament and council may no longer be regarded as essentially the same, what is our general conception of the former to be? It is hardly necessary to deal here with the various modern views since the days of Stubbs. The main ideas underlying the following brief and necessarily very incomplete examination of the problem may be stated at once. It will be seen that they are a reaction against the increasing tendency to find the essence of parliament in its judicial functions, to make the crowning institution of thirteenth and fourteenth-century England little more than a court of law. The essence of parliament, it will be suggested, was the act of 'treating' between the king and the nation, or those who were conceived as representing the nation, the "universitas regni."[1] The business of parliament was the "negotia regis et regni,"[2] the affairs of the state. An attempt will be made to show that this was the earliest conception of parliament, in the first half of the thirteenth century, and that no revolution of the traditional ideas is to be discerned until at least the reign of Edward II. Of course the personnel of parliament expanded in the second half of the thirteenth century, and the judicial functions of king and council within parliament became of very great importance under Edward I. But the expansion of parliament to include the commons was only a logical development of the traditional view of the assembly; and the addition of important judicial activities enlarged, but by no means transformed, its essential purpose in the state. It is not until the reign of Edward II that the commons find an integral and recognised place within parliament, in the sense that the name parliament will be officially withheld from an assembly to which they have not been called; and it is not until some period in the fourteenth century that the judicial activities of king and council are regarded, as in the *Modus Tenendi Parliamentum,*[3] as a necessary feature of a parliamentary assembly. They were recognised as natural and usual as early as *Fleta;*[4] but it seems probable that the king's ministers, even to the end of Edward I's reign, would not find it difficult to regard an assembly where no judicial activities took place as a parliament. The idea of parliament as an assembly in which the commons could petition for remedy of wrongs belongs essentially, it would seem, to the fourteenth century; it grew out of, but it would be a profound mistake to think that it ever really displaced, the old conception of the assembly as called essentially for solemn discussion between king and subjects on important matters of state. Different people had, of course, different conceptions, about this as about any institution. We are not concerned with these. There was, we would suggest, sufficiently established, a dominant, accepted, official view. This was probably modified and expanded with the passage of time; but it never, so far as contemporary documents will guide us, represented the medieval parliament as essentially a court of law.

We are not attempting to discover what were the actual activities of parliament at this period—these are very well known—so much as to find out what contemporaries believed the essential activities of a parliament ought to be. It is not of supreme importance, in this connection, to find out that judicial activities fill a large part of the Rolls of Parliament under Edward I: indeed, the official records of parliament are not of very great help. Some information is certainly conveyed by enactments like the Ordinances of 1311 and the Statute of York in 1322, and these are discussed below. But the greatest attention is given, in the pages which follow, to the writs of summons to parliaments and other assemblies, issued from chancery, and to the memoranda in the chancery rolls. It is much more important, for our purpose, to discover how the chancery officials distinguished a parliament from other general assemblies, than to know exactly what took place in parliament itself. We do not wish to analyse parliament alone, so much as in relation to and as distinguished from, other meetings of the "universitas regni" and the king. It seems probable that the formulae by which chancery summoned a parliament would express the official tradition as to what the essence of a parliament was; and that if we could discover the reasons why the chancery did not classify some general assemblies as parliaments, we should have obtained a valuable insight into the official definition of what a proper parliament ought to be. Hence much time has been spent, in the pages below, on the *tractatus* of Edward I and Edward II. All this has involved the assumption that chancery followed rules in its issue of writs and its official memoranda, rules which were both intelligible and fairly consistently observed; but this is not difficult, in view of the practice of chancery in other aspects of its work. It has also involved a good deal of speculation; but the result has been a picture of the working of chancery and the growth of parliament as reflected in the chancery records which, if it still presents many difficulties, seems to fit in very well with the evidence on the nature of parliament available, at this period, from other sources outside the chancery itself.

We cannot discuss here the question of the origin of parliament, or the nature of the early business. Valuable evidence has been collected by Mr. Richardson. The situation about the middle years of the thirteenth century may be summarised in his words: "This concern with what we may call politics was a feature common to all parliaments which have any claim to be called national, a characteristic to be discerned very much earlier than any attempt to use parliaments as a regular and ordered means of providing remedies for wrongs." We may conceive the parliaments of the thirteenth century as growing naturally out of the great assemblies of the Curia Regis of an earlier time. They were summoned because of the ancient tradition that the king could not change the laws or make major decisions concerning the welfare of his people without consulting his magnates. As Robert Grosseteste said about this time, "nec tam idiota sum quod credam ad alicujus suggestionem te vel alium sine principis et magnatum consilio posse leges condere vel commutare."[5] The favourite way of describing the activities of the magnates in these 'parliaments' was to say that they were summoned to 'treat' with the king: they had to agree about the step which the king proposed to take; and their agreement was of supreme importance, as it had been long before, when Rufus had sought their support against Anselm in 1095, or as it was when the barons declined to change the laws of England under Henry III. We may assume that the changing of law figured largely amongst the activities of this ancient assembly; but we may safely decide perhaps that, whatever parliament later became, its earliest importance does not seem to have been that of a court for remedying wrongs. If we may judge from the scanty evidence available, it seems to have been rather that of a forum in which the king and the magnates discussed and agreed upon the most important affairs of state.

There is no evidence that the conception of parliament became essentially different in the period 1258-65; indeed in this period we have two characteristic and important expressions of what we may perhaps venture to call the traditional view of the normal functions and personnel of a parliament. In the Provisions of Oxford we get very illuminating arrangements for the future holding of parliaments. As is well known, there were, in future, to be three parliaments a year. The functions of the parliaments were referred to: they were "pur treter de bosoingnes le rei et del reaume."[6] Parliament was, as has been pointed out, in all probability intended to discuss broad matters of state. To the barons in 1258, as far as we can tell, the judicial functions of a parliament did not exist. Parliament may have been, already, the place where some very important judicial processes took place; but this was not why the barons in 1258 demanded three parliaments a year. Similarly, the arrangements give us an illuminating insight into the baronial conception of the essential elements in the personnel of a parliamentary assembly in 1258. Parliament could be conceived as consisting of the king and council on the one hand, the twelve barons elected by the commonalty (*le commun*) on the other. The position of the king is ambiguous; clearly the articles of the barons were framed to give the council of fifteen the greatest possible measure of power, and they did, in effect, obscure the functions of the king. On the other hand, it would be dangerous for us to assume that the king was, or could be, altogether left out. King and council, we may perhaps assume, acted (as elsewhere provision is made that they should act) together, treating with the barons. Council and baronage were clearly distinct in parliament, even when the council was a baronial council. The twelve elected by *le commun* represented *tut le commun de la tere:*[7] they were elected only *pur esparnier le cust del commun.*[8] We know that *le commun* in effect, consisted, in 1258, of the magnates alone; but the language is not without significance. *Le commun* was a fortunate term for the barons, variable and elastic in its meaning. The arrangements of 1258, in spite of the aristocratic nature of the opposition at the moment, seem clearly to reflect a conception of parliament as a meeting place of king and *universitas regni,* discussing the weighty matters common to both. . . .

An immense increase in the judicial activities in parliament undoubtedly occurred during or before the early years of Edward I. This was, indeed, a change not confined to parliament, but paralleled by one which occurred somewhat later in the council. Perhaps, indeed, it should be regarded as an extension of the activities of the council in parliament, rather than those of parliament itself. It was probably due to a variety of causes; the two most important perhaps being the increasing practice of summoning representatives of the shire and borough to parliament, and a great increase of appeals to the king, due to the normal growth of legal actions, the growth of the power of precedent in the courts, and the increasing specialisation of different aspects of the Curia Regis. These appeals were to the king, not to parliament; they were offered in parliament as this was the most convenient time to approach the king. Parliament was not, so far as our evidence goes, summoned for this purpose; the knights of the shire and burgesses were first ordered to attend at a time before the judicial aspect of parliament had become an important one; and the cause of their summons seems to have been primarily that of finance, though undoubtedly their functions were considerably widened under Edward I and in subsequent years. But the king never summoned them especially to hear their petitions, or those of the lords; it was the business of the subject to approach the monarch for this purpose, not the monarch to summon the subject; and it seems probable that the king was accessible to petitioners outside the meetings of parliament, as well as within. The growing custom of using the meetings of parliament to approach the king for remedies was, indeed, clearly unwelcome to Edward I: "Pur ceo ke la gent ke venent al parlement le Roy sunt sovent deslaez et desturbez a grant grevance de eus e de la curt par la multitude des peticions ke sunt botez devant le Rey," the king said in 1280, "de queus le plus porroient estre espleytez par Chanceler e par justices, purveu est ke tutes les peticions ke tuchent le sel veynent primes al chanceler, e ceus ke tuchent le Escheker veynent al Escheker. . . ."[9] These petitions were not the essential work of the king in parliament, and the king was anxious to get them as far out of the way as possible. Yet were it not for these petitions, it does not seem probable that justice would ever have been regarded as the essential feature of parliament; the commons would have had no participation in the justice administered there at all.

Much importance has been attached to *Fleta's* description of parliament under Edward I as a place where judicial doubts are determined, new remedies are established for new wrongs, and justice is done to every one according to his deserts. But in the first place the writer of *Fleta* was obviously preoccupied with the judicial work of the assembly; we have no right to assume that he would have otherwise regarded it as equal in importance to the political. In the second place, much of the work was of a kind which would properly require discussion between the king and his subjects; if we would describe it by any modern term we should perhaps call it legislative rather than judicial. In the third place, though this is not important here, it was not parliament in the modern sense which performed this work; it was the king in his court "in concilio suo in parliamentis suis."[10] Making new laws would probably involve the participation of the whole assembly; but the vast bulk of the judicial work would be done by king and council. Parliament was *the assembly in which* this was done; the idea of parliament itself performing such functions belongs to a later age.

Edward I wrote of parliament as essentially a place for the discussion of matters of state, not as a court in the modern sense. "It is the custom of the realm of England," he wrote, "that in all things touching the state of the same realm there should be asked the counsel of all whom the matter concerns." He had caused the question of Peter's Pence to be reserved for deliberation in parliament, he told the Pope in 1275; but though he ordained many things for the amelioration of the state of the church and the realm, before he was able to conclude the parliament, by reason of the multitude of matters needing reformation, he fell ill and was unable to deal with that matter; he cannot answer now because he is bound by his oath not to do anything touching the crown of the realm, without the counsel of the *proceres.* Judicial matters were, as we have seen, regarded in 1280 as an impediment to such necessary debates. In his summonses to parliament he repeatedly showed that to him, at any rate, the main business of parliament was not judicial, whatever it was to his subjects, who unfortunately are inarticulate on the point; the mere fact that they presented petitions in parliament in no wise proving that they went to parliament primarily for that purpose. There is less tendency now than there was, perhaps, to minimise the importance of that famous tag of Edward's chancery— "quod omnes tangit ab omnibus approbetur, sic et nimis evidenter ut communibus periculis per remedia provisa communiter obvietur"[11], and it suggests the same conception of the business of the assembly. In summoning the clergy to the parliament of November 3rd 1296, the king said that in their last assembly at Westminster they had promised a subsidy unless peace should be achieved between England and France; he therefore summoned them to fix the amount of the subsidy. On another occasion parliament was summoned "Propter quedam specialia et ardua negocia nos et statum regni nostri tangencia que noviter emerserunt, et que sine vestra presencia nolumus expediri".[12] . . . Judicial activities were increasing greatly under Edward I; but we cannot say that there is evidence, even in *Fleta,* that the essence of a parliament was considered to be that of a court of law. The political and legislative functions of the assembly still seem to have been considered the essential ones. This may not have been the view of the increasingly important members of the commons, but it was the view of the government, the official view.

The same can be said, with some reserves which will be considered below, even for the reign of Edward II. Perhaps we may say of this reign that opinion was changing, but it had not yet changed. It would be very long, indeed, before the newer judicial functions of parliament would be regarded as equally essential with the old. The traditional view was still apparently expressed by Edward II in 1326 when he wrote: 'He wishes them [the chancellor and treasurer] to take his place on the first day [of parliament] ... and say that he will be there at the said time to treat on the business for which he has caused Parliament to be summoned.' He was assuredly not thinking of the hearing of petitions or remedying wrongs. The same view of parliament appears in the well-known letter of the Earl of Lancaster in 1317, in the treaty of Leake, and in the Statute of York in 1322.

The Ordinances of 1311 deserve a word to themselves. The famous clause 29 seems almost to have been regarded by some historians as defining the essence of a parliament; but in fact it did nothing so ambitious as this. In it the barons insisted that parliament should be held once or twice a year, in a convenient spot, so that cases might be heard in which the king was involved, and petitions considered. They did not say that this was the essential reason why parliaments should be held; and, indeed, other clauses show plainly that the barons were determined to have the most important political questions settled in parliament and not elsewhere. The Ordinances show us that the judicial functions had become so important as to receive the special attention of the barons in one of the great reforming projects of the time; but they do not in any way suggest that the magnates would have seriously maintained that parliament was essentially a court of law. We may, indeed, perhaps venture to regard the Ordinances as a landmark in the evolution of the judicial functions of parliament; as obtaining formal recognition for the judicial activities which we know had been vigorous in parliament since the early days of Edward I, and as possibly contributing towards making such activities, in future, a necessary feature of all parliaments, even though the Ordinances did not remain the law of the land. But they did nothing, so far as we can see, to diminish the traditional view of parliament as being primarily a political assembly; nor do they help us to judge how far contemporaries were really prepared to regard the more recently acquired judicial functions of parliament as being as essential to its proper existence as its long-established political ends.

Lastly, we have the important evidence of the *Modus Tenendi Parliamentum.* Parliaments are summoned firstly for war, if there should be a war, or other business touching the persons of the king, the queen or their children; secondly, for the common business of the realm, such as decreeing new laws after the giving of judgments which is pre-eminently common business; thirdly, there ought to be remembered the business of individuals, and this according to the order of the files of petitions. Modern research into the structure of parliament seems to confirm the view that the writer of the *modus* was perfectly familiar with the main outlines, at least, of parliamentary procedure in the fourteenth century. His testimony on the general nature of this procedure, and on the contemporary view of parliament, according as it does with all the other important evidence from the same and from the earlier period, must be given very great weight.

There is, it seems probable, no evidence of a transformation of the essential nature of parliament before the reign of Edward III. Its activities were broadening, and this is evident in the importance attached to the remedying of wrongs in parliament, in *Fleta,* as early as the reign of Edward I. By 1311 the judicial activities within parliament had clearly become established as a traditional feature of the assembly, of very great importance. But it still seems probable that, even to the Ordainers, the idea of parliament was the traditional one, the idea of a meeting of the "universitas regni" summoned to discuss affairs of state with the king. Have we any other means of throwing light upon contemporary opinion? There are, of course, the records of parliament, especially the Rolls of Parliament. The latter were, under Edward I, for instance, largely filled with records of judgments, answers to petitions; indeed, the two chief clerks of parliament were preoccupied with the enrolment of such answers. But this is hardly decisive. It was more important, for some reasons, to enrol a legal verdict, than to enrol a general assent to some proposal of the king; and a general discussion of much importance might afford little to enrol. One fact of great importance does emerge from a study of these records, and is commented on elsewhere. Parliament was not an enlarged council; its functions were not the same as those of king and council, demonstrably much engaged in answering petitions. The essence of a parliament we may reasonably conclude, in the light of what has already been said, was in the business over and above that arising out of the petitions themselves. This is, of course, entirely in accordance with the procedure of parliament, as far as this is reflected in the rolls. The king will explain, or have explained, the cause of summons, and this will take the form of business of state. Petitions will be accepted, but that is not why the assembly has been called. Normally the king will explain his needs, and ask for support. The business of answering petitions will be relegated to smaller committees; only the most exceptional or important cases will be allowed to come before 'parliament' at all.

These facts are mostly well known; they are, it is true, capable of being variously interpreted; but they seem on the whole to support the conception of parliament suggested above. One line of approach remains, which has not perhaps received, in recent years, the attention it deserves—the much debated and ambiguous 'parliamentary writ.' It is true that the nature of a parliamentary writ is very hard to define, and that the whole existence of such an instrument has been left in a state of considerable doubt by the latest historians of parliament in the period under review. But these historians themselves have cited a contemporary reference to the chancery practice which should serve to place the existence of a parliamentary writ almost beyond doubt. It is hard to believe, in any case, that the chancery, so meticulous in the wording of other writs, was casual and slovenly in the issue of the important letters under the great seal which summoned the formal assemblies going under the name of parliament in the reign of Edward I. It is much easier to believe that there was a parliamentary writ, but that the chancery officials did not always know exactly what kind of assembly was in fact contemplated by the king— whether or not it actually fell within the category of a 'parliament.' But these border-line cases which inevitably occurred need not serve to discredit all idea of the existence of a parliamentary writ. On the contrary, properly understood, they may give us an invaluable insight into the mind of the chancery official; they may teach us what he regarded as the essential qualities of a parliamentary assembly. His acceptance or rejection of an assembly as a parliament, in the rubric he made in the Rolls of Chancery, deserves the greatest consideration. If the chancery official who issued the order for an assembly did not know whether or not it was a parliament who should know? If the rubric entered opposite the enrolment of his writ had no relation to the real nature of the gathering, we may well despair of making anything of the references which were made to parliaments, by different persons and for different reasons elsewhere. It hardly seems worth while attempting, at this distance in time, to distinguish parliamentary from other assemblies.

If we may assume for a moment—on entirely *a priori* arguments it is true, but arguments which, to anyone thoroughly familiar with chancery practices, must have some force—that there *was* something more than vagary behind the formulœ, and memoranda of the chancery officials, how should we, from a preliminary survey of the writs and enrolments of the department, define a parliamentary writ? A parliamentary writ of the reign of Edward I, it seems possible to decide, was drawn up to mark out the assembly it summoned on three important points:

(a) The summons is to 'treat,' normally *tractare.*

(b) The recipient is to treat not with the king alone, and not with 'others of the council' (a normal summons to a council, or of a councillor) but with a body of other magnates, with an assembly which might, according to the ideas of the age be regarded as the *universitas regni.*

(c) The assembly is to treat, not on the king's business, but on business of the king and of the realm—*negotia regis et regni.* A parliament is, the writ implies, an assembly of the *universitas regni* treating with the king on the affairs of the king and the state.

An examination of the chancery enrolments and the writs of summons under Edward I, in the light of this tentative definition, brings out a fundamentally important fact. The chancery officials have normally used the term 'parliament' in the rubrics which they have inserted in the chancery rolls, only opposite those writs of summons which agree in all particulars with the definition of a parliamentary writ set out above. The importance of this is very great; it is hardly diminished by the fact that they have not thought fit to classify every assembly summoned by a chancery writ. The nature of the assembly may, in some cases, have been sufficiently set forth; in others it may have been in doubt through exceptional circumstances of the time. At any rate they have classified enough to make it fairly certain that there were systematic ideas and practices behind their classification—to make it extremely probable, at least, that there was such a thing as a parliamentary writ.

We are justified therefore, in attempting, on the basis of the parliamentary writ defined above, and of the rubrics of the chancery officials, the difficult task of drawing up a list of parliaments under Edward I. . . .

It not only seems probable therefore, we may conclude, that a *tractatus* was an assembly distinguished from a parliament, in the reign of Edward II; it seems probable that we may learn, from the attitude of the chancery officials towards it, something more of the development of parliament itself during these years. The first point, of cardinal importance, which obvious though it is, has perhaps not always been sufficiently taken into account, is that parliament was undergoing rapid change. The importance of the judicial functions, which is so strongly emphasised at the present time, and which is, indeed, very evident in Edward III's reign, in fact only received general and formal recognition during the reign of Edward II. It may be doubted how far the fairly modest position occupied by judicial functions in the *Modus* would have been conceded by chancery officials, at least, before the Ordinances of 1311, in spite of their importance in the eyes of a lawyer like the author of *Fleta* under Edward I, and in spite of their importance in the actual business of members of parliament in the earlier reign. We do not find any indication that the lack of judicial functions debarred an assembly from the name of parliament, in the chancery records, until the later years of Edward's reign, and even then the nature of the indication is not very sure. But it seems probable that the Ordinances of 1311 strengthened a tendency, already in existence, to look for these functions in a parliamentary assembly, and that this, accepted (somewhat grudgingly) by the *Modus*, would influence the clerks of chancery at least in November 1325.

Another feature of a normal parliament definitely established in these years was the presence of the commons. It seems probable that this was not necessary at the beginning of the reign: several undoubted parliaments do not seem to have included representatives of the boroughs and shires. It has been shown recently how the position of these became enhanced in the course of the reign; and they form an indispensable element according to the *Modus*, probably written in or near the reign of Edward II. We may perhaps venture to conclude that the absence of the commons would, in the later years of Edward II, be, for the first time, sufficient to render a major assembly, called to discuss affairs of state, no more than a *tractatus* in the eyes of chancery officials, and that this tendency would have been even more apparent in their records than it was, but for the critical circumstances which made classification such a difficult matter in 1325. It is certain that this principle, probably apparent in 1324, was universally observed in the early days of Edward III. . . .

By the end of Edward II's reign, it is clear that the general nature of parliament as the treating of king and *universitas regni* on matters of state has been implemented at many points. During the reigns of Edward I and Edward II both the functions and personnel of parliament have been largely transformed. Outside parliament, new institutions have been evolved to meet the increasing needs of government; the *tractatus* and *magnum concilium* of Edward I's and Edward II's reign have been created, as assemblies for debate, alongside parliament itself: they seem, indeed, now to stand in place of some of the types of parliamentary assembly of an earlier time. The new activities of parliament and the extended personnel combine to create the impression that there may have been, during this period, something more than an extension of function, on the part of parliament; that there may have been a change in the essential nature of the assembly; that this may, by the end of Edward II's reign, have become essentially and primarily a court, the High Court of Parliament, depending for its future importance and development mainly on its judicial powers. But this impression does not correspond to the facts; it is largely due to the misleading evidence of the records, which unintentionally exaggerate the importance of the judicial activities in parliament, by the bulk of the legal matter they contain. Though the *tractatus* and *magnum consilium* will perform some of the earlier parliamentary functions of discussion and debate, parliament itself will continue to stand essentially for the supreme co-operation of king and people in discussing and agreeing upon the highest matters of state. That this, and this only, is the ultimate basis on which its future development will take place, seems to be demonstrated throughout the whole of the period at present under review. We may be content at this point, perhaps, with the assertion that, so far as the evidence discussed above will take us, we may conclude that the more parliament developed, under the three Edwards, the more its essence seems to have been found in the general and unrestricted nature of both its activities and its personnel.

Notes

1. "University" or "community of the realm."–Ed.
2. "Business of the king and kingdom."–Ed.
3. "The Way of Holding Parliament," an English tract of the fourteenth century.–Ed.
4. *Fleta*, a legal treatise dating from the end of the thirteenth century.–Ed.
5. "Nor am I so foolish as to believe that you or someone else can establish or change laws without the counsel of the prince and the great men."–Ed.
6. "To treat of the business of the king and the kingdom." See Document G, p. 144.–Ed.
7. "All the community of the realm."–Ed.
8. "To spare the cost to the community."–Ed.
9. "Because people coming to the king's parliament are often deterred and disturbed, grievously for them and for the court, by the multitude of petitions brought before the king, of which most could be despatched by the Chancellor and by justices, it is provided that all the petitions concerning the seal come first to the Chancellor, and those that concern the Exchequer come first to the Exchequer. . . ."–Ed.
10. "In his council in his parliaments."–Ed.

11. See Document J. 1, p. 147, for a translation of the text from which these words (sentence two) are taken.—Ed.

12. "On account of certain special and arduous affairs touching us and the status of our realm, which have lately arisen and which we do not wish to settle without your presence."—Ed.

Part Three

ESTATES IN FRANCE

Chapter 7 ESTATES GENERAL: THEIR EMERGENCE UNDER PHILIP THE FAIR AND AUTHORITARIAN NATURE

For France, the problem was not so much
how incipient representative institutions
functioned, but when and why they arose
and why they failed to secure a firm hold in
the constitution. None doubted that the
Parlement of Paris (which arose simultaneously with its namesake in England) was
basically a court nor that the Estates-General
was a political assembly. CHARLES H.
McILWAIN (1871-1968), a distinguished
American historian of political and legal
thought, discussed the Estates General in
one of the first and best comparative
treatments of the rise of representation.
While he stressed the character of representation in the early Estates, his observations on
the background and character of these
assemblies were consistent with the prevailing views of French scholars.

It was to the appearance of a great national emergency, together with the continuance of . . . earlier institutions and practices, that we must attribute the unusual
developments in France in the time of Philip the Fair, which resulted in the first
assembling of the feudal estates on a national scale; and the inclusion in these
assemblies of the *bourgeoisie* was, in the first instance at least, due to the enfranchisement of so many of the communes during the thirteenth century, which thus
brought them within the feudal hierarchy and imposed upon them the burden of
the suit generally incident to feudal tenure whenever it was demanded of them by
their feudal overlord, together with the other customary obligations of *auxilium*
and military service.[1] In common with the other vassals of the king they owed him

From C. H. McIlwain, "Medieval Estates," *The Cambridge Medieval History*, VII (Cambridge,
E., 1932), 683-687, 690-692 (abridged; footnotes omitted). Reprinted by permission of
Cambridge University Press.

counsel and they owed him aid, and these, or the second of them at least, had been demanded and received by the kings of the thirteenth century from their *villes*, in assemblies of which the great lords had formed no part. The rapid differentiation in the central administration of the latter part of the thirteenth century is no doubt an important cause of this separate action. The judicial function of the old Curia had already passed in large part to the *Parlement*, while *consilium* had become one of the chief functions of the king's private council, though this was, as Viollet says, a matter of fact rather than of legal definition. When the communes were summoned, it was usually *auxilium* and that alone that was wanted, and before the opening of the fourteenth century, in all cases where it was demanded from them collectively, it was in assemblies to which no other feudatories were summoned. No doubt the reason why they had been summoned at all was the force of the feudal principle that all specific aids beyond the few accustomed ones could be assessed only with the consent of the vassals upon whom they fell. Instances of these separate assemblies of representatives of the *villes* are to be found a good while before the opening of the fourteenth century, and separate they might have remained much longer but for the great national questions brought up by the conflict between Pope Boniface VIII and Philip the Fair. For such a national emergency the old feudal revenues were inadequate. Feudalism was dying and its revenues drying up none the less surely, even if more gradually, than in England, and, as in England, the national power was rising and with it a national activity that required for its support a larger revenue than could be drawn from sources strictly feudal in character. The king was driven to treat on extra-feudal terms with his vassals, the barons and the enfranchised *villes*. Thus the estates are feudal, but they are extra-feudal also. Philip probably called to him in 1302 none who did not owe him feudal suit, but he did it in a way unprecedented in feudal custom. The departure from precedent might seem less striking in the occasional *assemblées de notables* to which none but great nobles lay or spiritual were summoned, but the greater assemblies of Philip the Fair were certainly an innovation, though their feudal basis is evident; and later meetings mark a far more radical departure from feudal institutions and ideas.

The first instance seems to have been in the year 1301 at an assembly held by Philip at Senlis, in which was demanded the counsel "clericorum et laicorum, doctorum *et aliorum proborum virorum,*"[2] on the difficult question raised by the king proceeding against the Bishop of Pamiers for breach of faith and *lèsemajesté*.[3]

But other differences arose between the Pope and the French King which finally became so serious that on 10 April 1302 Philip called a great meeting of the Estates at Paris. This assembly is usually regarded as the beginning of the States General, and the documents edited by the late M. Georges Picot enable us to draw with some confidence certain conclusions as to the character, powers, and activities of its members. The assembly was composed of tenants-in-chief of the king, lay and spiritual, as had long been the custom; and it also included *arrière-vassaux*,[4] "representatives" of enfranchised *villes*. All these *arrière-vassaux* were bound in a general way by the fealty they owed their liege lord, but direct negotiations with them were an addition to feudal custom which could be made regular only by the assent of their overlords who held of the king *in capite*.[5] In England, an aid had already been asked of the mesne lords, as we have seen, but "at the instance" of their feudal superiors. This was now done for France by Philip in 1302, and it illustrates the gradually widening basis of the State on both sides of the Channel, a process observable earlier in England than in France. In both, fealty is gradually becoming wider, more national, and less feudal, as wealth, power, and political self-consciousness diffuse themselves beyond the circle of the greater land-holders. But the development is a gradual one which proceeds without any distinct break with feudal custom. The mesne lords—a term including communes outside the royal demesne—are now summoned, but it is on account of an obligation which may be called as much feudal as national, and the innovation of summoning them is softened by obtaining the assent of the direct vassals who had hitherto concluded their tenants by their own unassisted decisions. This assent was forthcoming no doubt because the participation which was now first extended beyond the immediate circle of the king's tenants-in-chief was not a privilege to be guarded, but rather a burden which might be borne more easily when more widely shared.

Changing economic and social conditions were making increasingly difficult the older shifting of the incidence of the burden of *auxilia* sanctioned by regular feudal custom. The consent of the tenants-in-chief was necessary if such a change was to be made, but it was a consent probably not hard to obtain in view of the crisis which faced the nation in 1302. Thus it is clear that the basis of the membership of the first Estates was obligation and not right, an obligation arising out of fealty; while the growing forces of nationalism were now imposing upon it the necessity of direct negotiations between the king and his *arrière-vassaux*, hitherto unnecessary but now accepted by the chief tenants in the prospect of unusually heavy demands for aid in the impending struggle with the Pope, and accepted the more willingly no doubt because of their decreasing confidence in their ability longer to shift these burdens from their own shoulders to those of their tenants. That the real basis of the summons was obligation rather than right is made plain by the surviving summonses to the Estates themselves. In the very first of these, addressed by the king to the seneschal of Beaucaire on 15 February 1302, the purpose of the meeting is set forth in language which echoes the famous phrase of Edward I of England seven years before—"quod omnes tangit ab omnibus approbetur."[6] Since on "many difficult matters" which touch in no small degree the status and liberty of himself and his realm no less than of the churches, ecclesiastics, nobles, secular persons, and all and singular the inhabitants of the said realm ... the king wishes to "treat and deliberate" with his prelates, barons, and others the subjects and lieges of him and of the said realm, he commands to be summoned under their obligation of fealty and any other obligation whatsoever by which they are bound to him ... to appear at Paris on 8 April then next ensuing, the "consules et universitates civitatum et villarum praedictarum"[7] (in this case seven *villes*) through two or three "de maioribus et pericioribus singularum universitatum predictarum,"[8] who are to have full power from the aforesaid consuls and communes among other things "to hear, receive, and carry out, and to consent to everything ordained by the king in this regard without the excuse of a referendum," their presence being for the purpose "of treating and deliberating upon these matters, of hearing, receiving, and carrying out" all of them, and of giving their assent "in the name of the consuls and communes aforesaid" to all those things ordained by the king in the premises or connected therewith. The document here summarised clearly indicates that this summons grew out of the *obligations* incident to fealty. There appear also the instructions to "representatives" such as are to be found a generation earlier in England, but there is no definite reference to any election.

But an important question arises at the outset in regard to those things which touch the status and liberty of all the inhabitants of the realm. Must all actually approve of what touches all? Whom must the king include when he asks assent in matters thus touching all? How far beyond the prelates and barons does the obligation of fealty extend; or the additional phrase *quocumque vinculo*?[9] How much of this "representation" is only "virtual"? Shall we translate the important words "aliis nostris et eiusdem regni fidelibus et subiectis" with M. Picot, as "*les autres* sujets du royaume," or with the late Professor Esmein, as "*d'autres* fidèles sujets du royaume,"[10] thus including among the "others" none beyond the inhabitants of enfranchised *villes*? How far is this important experiment of Philip "national" and novel, how far is it merely feudal and traditional? It is a difficult question. There can be no doubt that there was a great development of these matters between 1300 and the great meeting of the Estates in 1484 for which Masselin's journal gives us such detailed information, but on the whole, though the paucity of documents for the first meeting makes certain conclusions impossible in regard to it, if we may judge from the history of earlier assemblies in France and elsewhere, the more conservative interpretation of Esmein seems to offer an explanation of these important transactions more in accordance with the facts and the political habits and ideas of the time than the "conséquences exagérées" of M. Picot. It is important, however, to bear in mind that this applies wholly only to the earliest meetings of the Estates.

Several times in 1303, at Paris, Montpellier, Nîmes and Carcassonne, and again in 1308 in the struggle with the Templars, the Estates were called together; and many of the documents have survived from which some conclusions may be drawn as to the general character of the assemblies in the early fourteenth century. They met again in 1314,[11] in 1356, when there were two assemblies, one for the South at Toulouse and one for the North at Paris;[12] in 1413 , and in 1484, and several times between; often in times of national defeat and civil disorder which make their actions seem more revolutionary than constitutional. The last meeting before the fateful one of 1789 was in 1614.

In the beginning the prelates and barons were required to appear in person, and such of the members of these assemblies as were ordered to come and gave their assent only *nomine consulum et universitatum*.[13] doubtless lacked many of the powers characteristic of the more fully developed representatives of modern times. The attendance of both classes was *sub debito fidelitatis*[14] and under threat of punishment for failure. But even the prelates and barons owing personal attendance might find it impossible to answer the summons in person, and in such cases they might appear by attorney, as was possible in all the royal courts at this time in both England and France, provided the royal licence could be had. The reasons given for these procurations or letters of attorney issued by the clergy for the meeting in Paris in 1303—here suspiciously numerous—which M. Picot has printed, shew conclusively that this appearance by attorney was at the time of that meeting regarded as an exception to be admitted only when sufficient cause was shewn. So one abbot prays this privilege "propter infirmitatem,"[15] the Prior of Saint-Léon of Sens is prevented from coming "gravi proprii corporis infirmitate."[16] "We have started on our journey," says another, "though very weak, but are not strong enough to appear in person, as God is our witness, without grave danger to our health." Another is so poor and so burdened with his duties at home that he begs to be excused. Another has got as far as Troyes but the journey is too much for a man of almost eighty. . . .

Such specific instances as these indicate far more clearly than any amount of detailed comment the nature and the extent of representative institutions and ideas in France at the opening of the fourteenth century. Several points seem clear. The attendance is not a right but a duty, and a duty imposed primarily by the obligation of fealty. Those summoned to appear in person must do so, at the beginning of the century at least, unless they have an excuse, of whose sufficiency the king will judge. With the king's permission they may in such cases appear by an attorney. This Esmein considers exceptional and existing only in 1302. Normally, he says, they might appear by proctor if they chose. This was certainly not the case, however, at the first meeting in 1303, but obviously soon became the general practice. Such proctors when appointed were attorneys or *mandatarii*,[17] and usually little more. They represented in most cases no one but their principal. They were his personal agents and bound none beyond him by their acts. . . . Collective bodies such as *villes* or chapters of necessity had to appear by a proctor or proctors, who were likewise regarded oftentimes as little more than *mandatarii*, as is indicated among other things by their being occasionally allowed to appoint substitutes, a power hardly consistent with the existence of the discretionary power necessarily incident to representation in any developed sense. But many cases go far beyond this. There were other proctors who were general as well as special, empowered in advance legally to bind their principals in any way whatsoever, and there were cases where several prelates or barons agreed to employ the same proctor in common, and one instance at least where several bishops of a single province are authorised to choose one of their own number "to act as representative in place of all and to have the full power of all." In the *villes* the developments are particularly interesting. For purposes of representation they are conceived in the usual manner of the time as collective wholes, *universitates* or communes, and the proctors they chose represent the *universitas*. Apparently the franchise is wide, and the decision is sometimes made by the vote of a majority. This body of the *ville* usually includes nobles and non-nobles, but in one case in 1308 there are two communes in a single *ville*, the nobles and the *populares personae*,[18] the second of which separately chose a proctor for their own *universitas*. Seemingly none but the inhabitants of the towns are represented in these assemblies of 1303 and 1308. The inhabitants of the open country are not mentioned till long afterward. . . .

Gradually the nobles and the prelates ceased to attend the meetings of the Estates in person or to be required to do so. It became their practice, contrary to that of England, to appear only by deputy; and a further step of the greatest importance followed when the prelates and the nobility of a general district began regularly to elect a small number of proctors to represent them all. Equally important was the extension of the franchise to the people of the whole *bailliage*[19] including the open country as well as the *villes*, as is found in 1484 at the meeting of the Estates at Tours. This was no doubt exceptional, but it seems to indicate the existence, temporarily at least, of conditions in some respects not greatly different from those in the English shire. Unlike England, however, the representatives of each order in the French districts were chosen, not by all the electors together as in the county court but separately, each of the orders, clergy, nobility, and "third estate" choosing deputies to represent none but their own order in the *bailliage* at the general meeting of the Estates. In 1484, in the case of the third estate, the suffrage for these elections seems to have been almost universal; but, taking the later Middle Ages in general, the basis remained on the whole municipal rather than general, though at times of crisis it was occasionally extended in theory at least to cover the whole *bailliage*. So, as Augustin Thierry says, however restricted may have been the representation of the third estate on account of its exclusively municipal character, it nevertheless had the merit of feeling itself charged with the duty of pleading the cause, "not of this or that fraction, nor of this or that class of the people, but the cause of the whole body of the non-nobles, of the people without distinction of free or serf, of bourgeois or peasant."

There were thus in 1484 deputies for and from each order or estate, but all represented one "electoral district"; and the *bailliage* for which they all appeared included the *villes* and, theoretically at least, the *campaniae*[20] as well. . . .

The French Estates in times of crisis exercised unusual and enormous power, as in 1420, and Glasson believes that it was the very extravagance of their acts at such times that caused their later weakness. But the reasons for this weakness, and for the long intervals between their meetings as compared with the frequent parliaments in England, lie much deeper and have their roots, some of them, in a past already distant in the fifteenth century.[21]

Notes

1. Cf. Document B, p. 142.—Ed.
2. "Of clergy and laymen, doctors *and other good men.*"—Ed.
3. Treason.—Ed.
4. Rear-vassals.—Ed.
5. In-chief.—Ed.
6. See Document J. 1, p. 147.—Ed.
7. "Consuls and communities of the aforesaid cities and towns [*villes*] ".—Ed.
8. "Of the greater and more experienced [men] of each of the aforesaid communities."—Ed.
9. "By whatsoever bond."—Ed.
10. "The other subjects of the realm" . . . other faithful subjects of the realm."—Ed.
11. See below, pp. 149, 79.—Ed.
12. For the summons to similar assemblies in 1345-1346, see Document N, p. 149.—Ed.
13. "In the name of the consuls and communities."—Ed.
14. "Under obligation of fealty."—Ed.
15. "On account of infirmity."—Ed.
16. "By the grave infirmity of my own body."—Ed.
17. "Those commissioned," "bearers of orders."—Ed.
18. "Ordinary persons"—Ed.
19. "Bailiwick"—Ed.
20. "Countrysides"—Ed.
21. McIlwain concludes with further comparative remarks; the comparison between France and England is illustrated p. 78 in the selection by Robert Fawtier.—Ed.

Chapter 8 PROVINCIAL ESTATES IN BURGUNDY ORIGINATE WITH ACQUISITION OF FISCAL AUTHORITY

JOSEPH BILLIOUD (1888-1963) was trained at the École des Chartes (Paris) and served for many years as Archivist-Librarian of Marseille. His solid study of the Estates of Burgundy, from which the present selection is translated, exemplifies a school of historiography which conceived of the history of medieval representation almost exclusively in terms of assemblies of the three orders possessed of constitutional attributes.

The Estates general or provincial of the Middle Ages are the direct ancestors of our parliamentary assemblies, the basis of representative government. By "provincial Estates" we mean an assembly regularly constituted by the reunion of deputies of the clergy, secular and regular, of the nobility, and of the towns of a given region. The levy of taxes in the Middle Ages was in principle dependent on the consent of these Estates; the sovereign, after a series of mutual concessions, gradually came to admit their intervention in the government of the region.[1]

The heads of ecclesiastical lordships—bishops, abbots, deans, priors, commanders—were convoked to the Estates not by reason of their dignity but as

From Joseph Billioud, *Les États de Bourgogne aux XIVe et XVe siècles* (Dijon: Académie des Sciences, Arts et Belles-Lettres de Dijon, 1922), pp. 7-17, 328-329 (abridged; footnotes omitted). Translated by editor. By permission of Académie des Sciences, Arts et Belles-Lettres de Dijon.

holders of fiefs, just as were the nobles. . . . What, in fact, was the role of the two privileged orders, immune from the taxes which, on behalf of their vassals, they were to grant to the duke, unless to defend the interest of those vassals against the deputies of towns on whom the fiscal burdens otherwise fell? Defending their men they protected themselves, for their interest was to see that their own revenues were not depleted. . . .

Unfortunately, the history of the Estates of Burgundy is that of an institution which has left testimonies so rare and dispersed that its parliamentary activity can only be examined in a spirit of profound modesty. Until the end of the fifteenth century . . . we know absolutely nothing about the . . . work of individuals as it bears on the . . . assemblies. . . . One is therefore limited to the study of the mechanism of the institution and to the minute analysis of tendencies that could have transformed an occasional assembly into an organ of representative government.

. . . The antiquity of the Estates of Burgundy has been exaggerated.[2] . . . If the three orders of the duchy are to be found this early, or earlier, it is in the assizes of the Parlement of Burgundy, then called the *"Grands Jours* of Beaune." This Parlement, detached from the *Curia ducis*[3] at the beginning of the thirteenth century, was still composed of the same members as the *Curia*, joined, when assizes were held, by inferior judges, such as bailiffs. . . . For important cases, or when the duke promulgated judicial ordinances, representatives of the three orders were summoned to these solemn assizes at Beaune . . . ; then, little by little, the representatives were eliminated from it,[4] and after 1353 one finds only practitioners in the legislative assizes, as in the properly judicial ones. This elimination corresponds to the period when the sovereign no longer required legislative counsel from the three orders, but only financial aid; when the separation of powers was becoming pronounced; and when there appeared the first Estates worthy of the term. . . . The old thesis of Mr. Dareste[5] who saw the Estates as emerging from the *Curia ducis*, associating town deputies in certain circumstances, thus seems applicable to the duchy of Burgundy. . . .

The association of the three orders of the duchy in 1314 was opposed to the exactions of Philip the Fair[6] who, for his wars of Flanders, had taxed the sale of provisions at six pennies per pound. While the number of deputies attending the judicial assizes is unkown, here we have a real assembly comprising a hundred nobles, twenty abbots, seven deans, eight priors and eleven towns. The latter were acting "for us and for all the towns, great and small, of the duchy of Burgundy"; this proves that the representation of the three orders of the province was complete in this case. A commission of six knights was appointed, whose work was to be made known to the dispersed deputies through governors of districts. The assembly was to be reconvened yearly at Dijon on Quasimodo Monday;[7] in this general session, the deputies would review measures already taken and deliberate on new ones; they would also renew the standing commission of governors. We should note that the towns made a point of specifying that they should have deputies in these assemblies, undoubtedly fearing that a right so novel would be contested. This general assembly of the three orders representing the duchy thus seems to have been unprecedented. And it was to have no consequence: for the Burgundians, satisfied with the charter won from Louis X[8] in April 1315, abandoned their parliamentary ambitions.

... Another fact confirms again the nonexistence of the Estates as a normal instiiution before 1352. It is well known that in 1335, instead of applying to the three orders, the duke caused an extraordinary subsidy to be asked of his subjects by commissioners traveling from town to town, according to a practice also known in the royal domain. But, on the other hand, was not this discretion itself a first step toward the convocation of Estates? It was a question, in this case, of an imposition not included among the four feudal cases,[9] and which thereby infringed the fiscal privileges which had been gradually established in the course of the thirteenth century. On account of political circumstances, the need of money increased, with the result that new and irregular taxes had to be levied; from that time on it became necessary to abandon the precarious system of occasional consultation and to have recourse to the Estates to remove pretext for local resistance. This was the only way the duke could give his detested exactions some semblance of legality. . . .

What distinguishes the assembly of 1314 from true Estates is that, instead of being convoked to render obligatory aid to the sovereign, it was spontaneous, protesting. Quite different was the meeting of 2 May 1352 at Dijon. That day four abbots and a canon, proctors for all the clergy, four nobles representing the nobility, and finally the deputies of thirteen towns, one for each, in the name of the Third,[10] delegated their powers to seven proctors, chosen from persons other than themselves, to refuse the six pennies per pound demanded by royal commissioners. It was as guardian of the young duke Philip of Rouvres and holder of his revenues that John the Good[11] made this request. This circumstance probably hastened the assemblage of Estates by several years, for a duke in his majority, less in need of money and especially one more careful with his own domains than a suzerain (foreign at that), would perhaps not have summoned them so soon. Thus the origin of the Estates of the duchy in 1352 resulted from the new requirements of the monarchy which, in view of the inadequacy of its ordinary domain resources, was compelled to seek the support not only of vassals of the royal domain but also of those of a province temporarily in his control. It was on the same basis that in December 1355 the king of France requested a *gabelle*[12] like the one he had obtained from the Estates general of the kingdom and thereby exposed himself in Burgundy to the repeated refusals of the year 1356. But in the following year, the Estates were more conciliatory because it was becoming necessary to provide for the defense of the region, and so began a series of continuous subsidies. Moreover, these subsidies were compensated by a series of concessions wrung from the duke by the three orders, which were to form the basic privileges of the region; that is why the principle of assemblies of Estates rests fundamentally upon mutual compromise.

In truth, the assembly of 1352 differs from the Estates of 1356 by the small number of members of the clergy and nobility; the latter acted not only in virtue of their own dignity, but as proctors of their entire order, which presupposes preliminary assemblies of these two orders and thus assimilates them better to the Third. If the word "Estates" is not used, the fact is that this designation was never constant. The assembly of 1352 merits the designation by its nature: while that of 1314 was only an occasion for meeting, that of 1352 became, on the other hand, the starting point for a new institution based, in reality, on old feudal elements and not created alone from royal initiative. The eagerness of the towns of the Third to respond to the royal appeal and the presence of villages like Saint-Thibault, Mont-Saint-Jean and Montréal betray, as in 1314, the novelty of their right corresponding to the somewhat tardy progress of the *bourgeoisie* in Burgundy.

We may note that the curious thesis of Mr. Callery on the origin of Estates[13] is inapplicable to Burgundy. According to him, Estates were convoked in consequence of extra-feudal measures . . . such as the payment for dispensation from military service. Incapable of innovating, the sovereign must apply to his vassals who, on the other hand, cannot refuse to pay him the price of a strict obligation: the conditions of the aid, but not the aid itself, become their right to determine. Now such a conclusion would be false for the Estates of the duchy, which always preserved the right to refuse the ducal request.

The term: "Estates." Instead of this generic term, first met with on 14 January 1356, it was usual to enumerate the parties, especially in solemn acts like the treaty of Guillon concluded in 1360 with the invader of the duchy, Edward III, king of England, and signed by the duke after consulting "prelates, nobles and communes." John the Good expressed himself likewise, as if fearing, in official acts, to pronounce the word "Estates," associated with such tragic memories for the monarchy. This usage, fairly constant in the fourteenth century, persisted in the fifteenth in the subscription of acts emanating from the Estates themselves.

. . . One can distinguish three grand epochs in the history of the medieval Estates of Burgundy: 1356 to 1382, 1383 to about 1441, 1442 to 1500.

The first period is marked by surprising activity: 63 convocations in 26 years; the second by a series of modest advances, hastened especially after 1430 (only 37 convocations from 1383 to 1429 . . . , then 30, one after another, in 10 years). With the third period, 94 sessions in 59 years, the institution attains maturity. Henceforth the frequency of assemblies no longer corresponds to fluctuations in the authority of the Estates, becoming rather the expression of the exterior situation and administrative needs. This does not mean that the Estates did not undergo certain vicissitudes, to which they were exposed more than other institutions by the very principle of their constitution. For the right of consenting to taxes never fully lost the defect of its origin, that of an imposition understood to have been the commutation of obligatory military service. Thus the two opposed principles were balanced, with one or the other prevailing by turns according to events and the power of the rulers.

Notes

1. This account echoes the influential definition given by Léon Cadier, *Les États de Béarn* ... (Paris, 1888), p. 1: "By "provincial Estates" we mean the reunion of the three orders of a province in a regularly constituted assembly, periodically convoked, and possessing certain political and administrative rights, chief of which is the vote of taxes."–Ed.
2. Here Billioud discusses certain assemblies of the later thirteenth century, dismissing them from consideration as not being composed of all three estates.–Ed.
3. "Duke's court,"–Ed.
4. I.e., from the Parlement.–Ed.
5. Billioud cites O. Dareste de la Chavanne's *Histoire de l'administration en France* ... , I (Paris, 1848), 79.–Ed.
6. King of France (1285-1314).–Ed.
7. I.e., the second Monday after Easter.–Ed.
8. King of France (1314-1316).–Ed.
9. I.e., subsidies admitted by custom on occasions when the lord knighted his eldest son, married his eldest daughter, went on crusade or had to be ransomed. "Extraordinary" subsidies were taxes not justified by the "ordinary" prerogative of the ruler, and therefore subject to the consent of those asked to pay.–Ed.
10. I.e., "Third Estate"; Billioud here refers back to the fourteenth century a conception only common much later in the Ancien Régime.–Ed.
11. King of France (1350-1364).–Ed.
12. Salt tax.–Ed.
13. Billioud cites Alphonse Callery, *Histoire de l'origine des pouvoirs et attributions des États généraux et provinciaux* ... (Brussels, 1881), pp. 28, 60.–Ed.

Chapter 9 ESTATES NOT USUALLY "PROVINCIAL" NOR EFFECTIVELY CONSTITUTIONAL

One of the few historians to perceive the defects in describing Estates as provincial assemblies of the three orders possessed of constitutional rights was GUSTAVE DUPONT-FERRIER (1865-1956), a specialist in the administrative history of France. In a review of Henri Prentout's book on the Estates of Normandy, the latter published in 1925-1927, Dupont-Ferrier was pleased to find Prentout preferring a more fluid definition of Estates than Cadier's, although he criticized Prentout on other points. He also took the occasion to survey the results of much other work on the "regional Estates," as he argued they should be called. Whether on specific points, concepts or general perspective, his remarks are in interesting contrast with Billoud's account of the Estates of Burgundy.

. . . In speaking of "provincial Estates" in the fourteenth century, we speak today not as one spoke in the time of the Hundred Years' War, but as one did after the Wars of Religion. . . . It would be better to say "regional" or "local" Estates prior to the sixteenth century.

The history of a word has its interest; but the origin of an institution is more important. How, it has been asked, did the "provincial" Estates begin?

As they appeared toward the end of the thirteenth century and especially in the fourteenth; while feudal France became more and more monarchical France; as the clergy and lords had to take account of the townsmen and their wealth; finally, as the menace of an Anglo-French state on both sides of the Channel was the gravest

From G. Dupont-Ferrier, "De quelques problèmes historiques relatifs aux 'États provinciaux,'" *Journal des Savants* (Aug.-Oct. 1928), pp. 315-357 (abridged). Translated by editor. By permission of Académie des Inscriptions et Belles-Lettres (Paris).

of perils for the realm of the *fleur de lys;*—it was natural to seek causes for these regional assemblies in feudal, monarchical, social, and external . . . matters.

Every great feudatory, it has been said, associated his principal vassals, lay and clerical, who owed him the service of court, counsel and aid (military or financial), the aid of *ost*[1] or *auxilium exercitus.*[2] The expanded feudal *curia* is thus supposed to have given birth to the "provincial" Estates. Dareste, Cheruel, Achille Luchaire so explained the appearance of the Estates. Callery emphasized the conversion of service into money, beginning with Philip III's expeditions to Spain. More recently, Mr. Duvernoy for Lorraine, Mssrs. Bougenot and Billoud for Burgundy, and Mr. Denizet for Provence, like the monographs on the Estates of Brittany, have sought to derive the new regional assemblies from these old seigneurial traditions.

Other scholars have seen the creation of these Estates as a work of the monarchy: thus, Mr. Antoine Thomas for central France, Mr. Dognon for Languedoc, the Abbé Dussert for Dauphiné, and now Mr. Prentout for Normandy. There would thus be a certain analogy between the blossoming of "provincial" Estates and that of "general" Estates of the kingdom. And the crown would have urged the development of regional assemblies because it judged them to be more manageable . . . than the grand assemblies.

. . . The progressive ascent of the popular and urban elite to material prosperity, judicial culture, administration, and government also helps to explain the place occupied by townsmen in the regional assemblies. Mssrs. Cadier, Dognon, Dussert and Hirschauer have emphasized this point.

The struggle of the Capetians against old feudal forces and the accelerating progress of the *bourgeoisie* were complicated by the difficulties of Philip the Fair, his sons and the first Valois kings with the English Plantagenets. To the necessities of interior politics and peace were added those of foreign policy and war. The more France was extended, the more it was exposed: to defend it, more copious resources than before were needed. Seigneurial custom, adjusted to the security of the fief, were inadequate to provide for the security of the whole kingdom. Even when he resorted to his suzerain rights, the king had to reinforce them with his sovereign rights, and so, to transform them. Feudalism, in France, had created several states. Now a single state was to take their place.

It was chiefly to obtain financial support, in connection with its new political needs, that the monarchy was to have recourse to the "provincial" Estates. With the consent of lay lords, clergy and common people, the king could obtain what he required as long as he could justify his request by a sincere and persuasive explanation of the general danger. The assemblies so convoked would discuss the question. But if they were deliberative bodies, they were also paying bodies.

So it was that by tact and persuasion the king could obtain what the feudal customs were legally entitled to deny him. He judged it more adroit to sollicit in particular from the various regional Estates what as a whole the so-called Estates general would perhaps have hesitated to grant him. With each of the regional

Estates he could have it recognized that the sums voted were conceded to him only by exception, for once only, without prejudice to the future. . . . If the feudal traditions or monarchical rights had sufficed to justify the king's claims, the "letters of non-prejudice" that he granted in this connection would have been useless.

It is clear, therefore, that the so-called provincial Estates are neither exclusively feudal nor exclusively royal; these Estates arise neither from suzerain nor from sovereign rights alone. . . . They develop from a new situation in which repeated negotiations were necessary.

And if some of these regional assemblies appear more nearly feudal in origin, others more nearly royal, that was the result of local differences, still very pronounced.

Consequently, before investigating the origin of the "provincial" Estates, it is necessary to study the origin of each in particular: what is true of some will not be true of others. It may be that in Languedoc or in Normandy the monarchy's influence was paramount, in Burgundy or Brittany, feudalism's. Each region preserved its own physiognomy and personality.

Diverse in origin, the Estates were even more diverse in their territorial structures: there were feudal districts (duchies of Burgundy or Lorraine, or of Normandy, Brittany or Guienne; counties or duchies of Anjou, Touraine; counties of Flanders, Artois, Champagne, Maine, Poitou, Angoumois, Rouergue, Béarn Foix, or Provence); administrative districts (in Languedoc); ecclesiastical districts (dioceses of Bourges, Chartres, Mende, Le Puy, Viviers); urban districts (Lille, Douai, Orchies, Lisieux, Falaise, Caen, Evreux, Coutances); peculiarly geographical districts (upper and lower Auvergne, upper and lower Limousin, Dauphiné, Navarre, Saintonge, Vexin); etc.

Nor were these districts immutable or rigid: sometimes the Estates of Normandy corresponded to the duchy, sometimes to the ecclesiastical province of Rouen, or for that matter, to some part of this duchy or province. For example, in 1346 were assembled the "Estates of the Norman tongue." Sometimes the Estates of Languedoc were limited to administrative districts, of which Toulouse, Carcassonne and Nîmes were the capitals; sometimes they added to these regions Rouergue, Albigeois, Gévaudan, Vivarais, Velay. . . .

. . .One thing is certain: between the second third of the fourteenth century and the second third of the fifteenth, there were few regions[3] in France lacking their local "Estates." At a time when the needs of war were demanding great sums of money, the king constantly appealed for the financial cooperation of the realm. The awakening of patriotism, the universal desire for security and the encouragement of the crown made these tragic years the golden age of what are called the provincial Estates. In spite of regional diversities, this institution became known everywhere in France.

This progress did not, however, result in the direct representation of the majority of the people in the Estates. In principle, only the upper classes, clergy and nobility as well as urban notables, took part. That is to say, the great masses of the region—people of the *"plat pays"*[4]—were excluded. The interests of villagers were supposed to be looked after by the lords, clerical or lay, on whom they depended.

A precise definition has been sought for these assemblies, and that of Léon Cadier has become well known. They are, he observed, "the convocation of the three orders of a province in an assembly regularly constituted, periodically convoked, and possessed of certain political and administrative attributes, chief of which is the vote of taxes." In 1923 Mr. Charles Hirschauer, in one of the most remarkable of the monographs devoted to the regional Estates, once again adopted this "brief formula" and called it "classical."

Mr. Prentout does not adopt it, however, and for reasons we find excellent. He rightly remarks that Cadier's definition could only apply to the moment when the "Estates" have attained their full development. It does not work for the period of their genesis and early evolution. Were it to be taken literally, there could not have been Estates in Normandy before 1423, perhaps not before 1458. "A medieval institution never arises fully developed from a constitutive act."

Let us add that Cadier was wrong to believe that these assemblies had a "province" for their setting. Except for ecclesiastical districts, there were no "provinces" in the fourteenth century. Until the middle of the following century, only the literary language spoke—although rarely—of provinces; the administrative language makes no mention of them.

Nor did the "three orders" always figure in the Estates called provincial. Mr. Hirschauer gives us more than one proof: for April 1364, October and November 1379, April 1393, February 1412, September 1415, etc. Yet these assemblies, often lacking the two privileged orders, are considered as "Estates" held in Artois by their learned historian.

In Dauphiné . . . the clergy was not really represented, and less still the "commons," except during a part of the reign of Charles VI. The nobles alone held the seats and influence. In Vivarais, the clergy was missing. Deputies were recruited exclusively in the other two classes, half in the nobility and half in the commons. In Languedoc as in Normandy, the deputies of the towns were generally masters in the assembly.

Even so, we cannot agree with Mr. Prentout that the Estates were democratic. Even when the urban element was preponderant, it was composed of an oligarchy of notables.

And above all let us avoid talking prematurely of the "Third Estate." It is only from the time of Louis XI that this expression begins to appear, in Normandy or elsewhere. And even then it was only in the sixteenth century that this locution came to prevail . . . contemporary with the arrival of the word "province."

. . . In summary, we find some solutions to historical problems suggested by the monographic study of the "provincial" Estates.

The term, which is an anachronism, was not applied to them before the second half of the sixteenth century. Better to call them "regional Estates." Their origins are very complex: old feudal traditions and, even more, the new needs of the monarchy contributed to their formation. But each of them retained its appearance and character. Their territorial settings were, likewise, variety itself: feudal, administrative, religious, urban, etc. And within these structures there was not rigidity: they incessantly expanded or contracted. Probably the monarchy had a part in this mobility.

Like their settings and their origins, the composition of these Estates differed a good deal depending on the region. The three orders were very diversely represented in them. But even where the towns were predominant, the Estates were by no means democratic. An oligarchy of notables, noble or *bourgeois*, was preponderant.

. . . Finally these regional Estates were never a serious or durable threat to the unity of the kingdom. They simply served to ease the transition between the feudal monarchy and the absolute. They might have contributed to the establishment of a limited monarchy, yet nothing came of that. As long as the crown had need of them, it admitted the principle of consent to taxation. But once the English peril ceased, it no longer felt a need to humor them: it provoked their decadence. They had aided the king, the king did not help them. He no longer tried to support those who had supported him. Their golden age ended with the Hundred Years' War: at the moment when the kingdom had just been reconquered, not so much for the French as for the king of France.

Notes

1. "Army" (i.e., "host").—Ed.
2. "Aid of the army." Cf. Document B, p. 142.—Ed.
3. The French word used here is *pays*—Ed.
4. "Countryside."—Ed.

Part Four COMPARATIVE APPROACHES

Chapter 10 ORIGINS AND COMPARISONS: THE CONCEPTUAL PROBLEM

Guizot had not been alone in recognizing that representative institutions had arisen everywhere in medieval Europe. But the combined influences of specialization and nationalism caused the wider perspectives to drop out of sight in the later nineteenth century; only after the First World War were they revived. In what follows, one of the greatest historians of the twentieth century argues that to explain the origins of representative institutions, one must look to the general or comparative circumstances in which they arose, that only by so doing could local investigators realize the full significance of their subjects. MARC BLOCH (1886-1944), who died in the French Resistance in World War II, wrote *French Rural History* (1931) and *Feudal Society* (1939) and founded a new school of social history.

Everyone knows what is meant by the Estates General or Provincial in 14th and 15th century France. (I use these epithets in their ordinary and approximate sense as a matter of convenience, without of course failing to be aware that the Estates General and Provincial were somewhat indeterminate bodies, that a truly 'general' Estates was practically never summoned, and finally that provincial representation was by no means fixed over a considerable period.) In the course of the last few years a number of monographs have been written on the Estates Provincial, especially those of the great feudal principalities. They represent an effort on the part of scholars that is all the more praiseworthy, seeing that almost everywhere, especially

From Marc Bloch, "A Contribution toward a Comparative History of European Societies," *Land and Work in Mediaeval Europe*, tr. J. E. Anderson (London: Routledge and Kegan Paul, 1967), pp. 54-56. Reprinted by permission of Routledge and Kegan Paul, Ltd., and University of California Press.

for the earlier period, the documents are appallingly scanty and barren of information. These monographs have cleared up a number of important points in a most
interesting manner. But from the very start almost all their authors have come up
against a difficulty they had no means of overcoming, the nature of which they
sometimes did not even recognise—I mean the problem of 'origins'. I am quite ready
to use this expression as ordinarily employed by historians; but though current, it is
ambiguous. It tends to confuse two intellectual operations that are different in
essence and unequal in scope. On the one hand there is research into the oldest
institutions (ducal or hundred courts, for example), out of which the Estates seem
simply to have developed. This is a perfectly legitimate and necessary enquiry. But
there remains the second procedure—namely research into the reasons that could
explain why, at a given moment, these traditional institutions took on a new lease
of life and a new significance, why they became transformed into Estates; that is
into assemblies endowed with political and financial duties, who were conscious of
possessing, over against the sovereign and his council, a certain power, subordinate
perhaps, yet none the less distinct, which was the ultimate expression, through
infinitely variable means, of the different social forces in the country. To bring the
seed to light is not the same thing as to show the causes for its germination. Might
we then hope to discover these causes if for instance we live in Artois (so far as the
estates of Artois are concerned) or in Brittany (if it is a question of the Breton
Estates), or even if we are content to take a general look at the kingdom of France?
Certainly not. This procedure would simply land us in a maze of little local facts, to
which we should be inclined to attribute a value that they certainly never possessed;
and we should inevitably miss the essential point. For a general phenomenon can
only be produced by equally general causes; and if there is such a thing as a
phenomenon occurring thoughout Europe, this—which I have called by its French
name, the formation of the Estates—is undoubtedly a case in point.

At varying moments—all, however, very close to one another in time—*Estates*
may be observed springing up throughout France; but in Germany too, in the
territorial principalities, there were the *Stände*[1] (the two words are curiously alike
in meaning), in Spain the *Cortes*, in Italy the *Parliamenti*. Even in the English
Parliament, which was born in a vastly different political environment, development
was often subject to a trend of ideas and a series of needs analogous to those which
led to the formation of what the Germans call the *Ständestaat*.[2] Please do not
misunderstand me. I fully recognise the immense value of local monographs, and I
do not in the least suggest that their authors should step outside the framework of
their proper studies and follow one another in a search for the solution to this
large-scale European problem that I have just referred to. On the contrary, we beg
them to realise that they could not, each one working on his own, find a solution to
it. The chief service they can do us is to uncover the different political and social
phenomena in their respective provinces which preceded or accompanied the
appearance of the Estates of the *Stände*, and which would therefore seem to have

some provisional claim to be numbered among its possible causes. In this enquiry, they would do well to pay some attention to the results obtained in other regions—to engage in fact in a little comparative history. The overall comparison would have to come later. Without preliminary local research it would be useless; but it alone will be able to select from the tangle of conceivable causes those which exercised a general effect—the only real ones. . . .

Notes

1. "Social condition" or "class."—Ed.
2. 'State composed of classes.' See the selection by Émile Lousse, pp. 87-91.—Ed.

Chapter 11 PARLIAMENT AND ESTATES GENERAL: THEIR DIVERGENCE EXPLAINED

ROBERT FAWTIER (1885-1966), professor
at the Sorbonne for many years, edited, or
directed the editing, of numerous volumes of
Capetian registers and fiscal accounts besides
publishing major studies in political and
institutional history. Few scholars were so
well versed in the intricacies of later
medieval government in France. In the
following selection, Fawtier compares the
practical realities of French and English
governments and societies to explain why
the histories of the Estates General and the
parliament moved in such different direc-
tions.

... This is not the place to repeat, after Pollard,[1] the description of a session of the
English parliament: the king enthroned facing, on their wool sacks disposed in a
rectangle, his counselors, chancellor, judges, barons of the Exchequer, with the
Lords spiritual and temporal seated not far from him, and around this Council and
at the end of the hall, when they were to be informed of the decisions taken by the
Curia in consilio,[2] those who will later be the commons of England ...

It is less easy to describe a session of the Estates General of France in the Middle
Ages. Its history is much less well known than that of the English parliament, the
documentation ... often inadequate.

Nevertheless, we have an extremely curious text which tells us of the assembly at

From Robert Fawtier, "Parlement d'Angleterre et États Généraux de France au Moyen Age,"
Comptes-rendus de l'Académie des Inscriptions et Belles-Lettres (1953), 276-284 (abridged).
Translated by editor. By permission of Académie des Inscriptions et Belles-Lettres (Paris).

Paris of August 1314. This text is found in the *Grand Chronicles of France* under the title: "Concerning the tallage and *maletoute*[3] imposed in France by Enguerran de Marigny," and reads as follows:

In this year [1314], on the feast of St. Peter, 1 August, Philip the Fair, king of France, assembled numerous barons and bishops at Paris; and in addition he caused burghers of each city of the kingdom to be summoned. When they were assembled in the palace of Paris on the day aforesaid, Enguerran de Marigny, knight, coadjutor to King Philip of France and governor of the whole kingdom, mounted a platform, at the king's order, with the king and the prelates and the barons who were sitting there on the said platform, where he was manifest to all, and preached to the people there before the platform as well as to the prelates aforesaid, making known the king's need and why he had caused them to come and convene.

(There follows Marigny's speech on the troubles with Flanders.)

Wherefore the said Enguerran on behalf of the king told the burghers of the communes assembled there that he wanted to know which of them would give him aid, or not, to mount a army against the Flemings in Flanders. And as Enguerran said this, his lord the king of France arose from his seat to see those who wanted to grant him aid. Then arose Stephen Barbete, burgher of Paris, and spoke for the said town, and represented the townsfolk, saying that they were all ready to give him aid, each as he was able, and even according to possibility, to go where he would lead them, at their own expense, against the said Flemings. And so the king thanked them. And after the said Stephen, all the burghers who had come there for the communes, responded that they would willingly give him aid, and the king thanked them.

One observes from reading this text how similar things were on both sides of the Channel. At Paris as at Westminster, it is the Council which deliberates, which decides, and those not of the Council are there simply to hear the decision and to furnish the means of execution.

Had the state of affairs described by the *Grand Chronicles* persisted, had there been assemblies every year like that of August 1314, it is not impossible that the institution might have developed in France as it did in England. But it did not happen so, and the reasons for the rarity and apparent disinterest in Estates General are easy to understand. France, it cannot be repeated too much, is the largest kingdom in Christendom in the Middle Ages. It is also the most populous kingdom. From the frontiers to the capital the distances are great and it is not easy to ask the southern towns to send delegates to the Estates General at Paris every year. Moreover, it was fortunate that such a demand was not made, for if all the 'good towns' of France had sent proctors or representatives to the Estates, it would have been hard to find a place where they could all meet. The dimensions of buildings in that period would not easily have afforded them an assembly-hall. And even had a large enough room been found for all the delegates, it would have been hard to make oneself understood for reasons of language, the southerners speaking another tongue from men of the north. Moreover, the length of the journey would have obliged the delegates to abandon their usual occupations, would have resulted in expenses for the towns sending them: expenses current from the moment of their departure and which, given the distances, would have risen considerably to cover many days. Finally, why should the communes or towns have wished to participate in assemblies where their participation was limited purely and simply to ratifying the decisions taken by the king and his Council, decisions strictly financial relating to the levy of subsidies? Since one had to consent sooner or later, there was no reason on that account to give up one's business and leave the shelter of the home town to run the very real risks that attended travel at that time. Was it not simpler to have the nearest royal agent indicate the amount to be paid and so to economize on money, energy and time? Besides, was it not better to hear this order from a lesser agent than from the king, sitting in the midst of his Council, in all his glory and in all his majesty? Was it possible to negotiate with this nearly divine personage, who cured the sick, who was consecrated with the holy oil of Reims, and whose veins carried the blood of Saint Louis? Clearly not. All that one could do in his presence was to prostrate oneself and even, perhaps, thank him for not asking for more.

It was not the same with the local royal official. He was someone who was known, who knew you, and knew the possibilities of the resources to be taxed; who would recognize that excessive pressure would only make it harder to levy the tax imposed, which in turn would expose him to displeasure of the monarchy for his failure. In the very interest of a good collection, it was better to arrange things at a lower level. The directives of the central authority could be adjusted in practice to the knowledge of local circumstances.

For all these reasons, it can be said that there were never true Estates General in France. There were only assemblies of representatives from a larger or smaller part of France: Estates General of Languedoc, Estates General of Languedoïl, and more often Estates of Normandy, of Vermandois, of Champagne, of Berry, of Limousin, etc. In principle, the king did not preside over these Estates. First, because it was difficult for the king to be everywhere at once; then, too, because, not wishing to risk a setback, he could not normally negotiate with his subjects. Therefore, it is commissioners appointed by him who convoke the Estates as needed, who represent the crown; but in a form less majestic, more human, one in which the simple mortals who are the subjects can more easily arrive at the compromises which are, in the Middle Ages, the very essence of the art of government.

Thus all sorts of reasons militated in favor of local assemblies in France. Moreover the royalty itself had an interest in avoiding oversized assemblies, where indiscipline threatened, where the mass of subjects might realize their own power. . . . It should also be recognized that the first attempts at Estates General, at a moment when the crown was weakened, were scarcely such as to encourage the king to have further recourse to them. Much is said of the Estates General of 1355-1358. But what is never said, perhaps because it is assumed to be known by all, is that even these Estates General of 1355-1358 represented northern France alone; that they were only Estates General of Languedoïl; that the Estates of Languedoc met at Toulouse independently of those at Paris, which, indeed—to a certain extent—they helped to oppose. We can understand why the royalty, after this experience, would have avoided, as much as possible, assembling the Estates at Paris again. It preferred the provincial Estates, convoked and managed by royal agents.

The situation was quite different in England. It has often been stressed that the English wanted a parliament. The men of 1258[4] wanted three each year; those in the time of Edward II wanted at least two. As Pollard well remarked, they would not have formulated such requests if the English parliament had been simply an occasion for voting subsidies to aid the royalty in its projects. The English parliament was something different. It was, above all, a High Court of Justice. It was there that subjects or communities of the kingdom presented their petitions; in this way some affairs were expedited, and, above all, this was a way of accelerating the course of justice. That is why the English felt they could not have enough parliaments, wanting at least three of them a year. On the other hand, medieval England was a very small kingdom, from which representatives could be assembled without difficulty. Moreover, one may ask who sat in parliament, so as not to be deceived by words and to speak prematurely of the House of Lords or House of Commons, thus reading back into remote centuries the Victorian reality . . . England is small, to repeat. A French bailiwick covered a considerable territory that was never perfectly defined. There does not seem to have been communal life in the bailiwick, the bailiff holding itinerant assizes in this miniature realm. An English county is smaller, more united. The people of a given county knew one another, associated easily in the county court in its frequent and periodic meetings. It was possible for that county to be so represented that no one would protest. We may also recall the happy formula of . . . Sir Frank Stenton, who defined England as a "kingdom created by conquest, organized for defense." Such a kingdom is composed of unities having, so to speak, an *esprit de corps*, representing topographical realities and not merely simple administrative divisions more or less artificial. When the king of England convokes his Council, he convokes . . . without difficulty what the king of France can do only when he convokes assemblies of nobles in the different bailiwicks of his kingdom. There were almost as many noble fiefs owing military service in the province of Normandy alone as in all the realm of England. There again, as everywhere, figures the question of dimensions. So too, when the king of England wants to convoke the deputies of his towns, the task is relatively easy: the English towns are not very numerous, the king knows them all. Let us not forget that the king of France, till almost the end of the Middle Ages, did not know how many towns, parishes, church towers he had in his kingdom.

And so, on the one hand, a small united kingdom, united since its birth; on the other a kingdom which seemed immense, and which had grown little by little through the reunion of very large feudal principalities, each with its institutions, customs, and peculiar life. The evolution of the English parliament and that of the French Estates General, so different from each other, resulted from that. And there is yet another factor: ... like the Estates General ..., the parliament of England could only be convoked by the king. But that was the limit of the resemblance. For if the king's presence was indispensable to the validity of the work of an English parliament, the Estates could assemble—and usually did assemble—under the presidency of royal commissioners. . . . Between the king and his parliament in England there was a far closer bond than between the king of France and his Estates General.

England being a small country, the fact that parliament is convoked frequently and regularly means that those who attend are almost always the same. Attending regularly, they will learn their trade, obtain their parliamentary education, something that will not happen in the Estates General. Finally, since ... the English counties were real political units ..., it will be possible to require them to delegate men to the parliament of the kingdom. There one will find men trustworthy, not burghers but knights, some of whom have all the necessary qualifications to be convoked individually to parliament by the king. It is they who are asked to accept or refuse the requests for subsidy addressed by the crown to its subjects. They come to parliament with full power to respond in the name of the county. This was not the case with the representatives sent to the Estates General. The latter came without power to hear and consent to what the king demanded. Hence their acceptance—or their submission—does not seem to have engaged their constituents. Once the subsidy was decided in the Estates General, it was still necessary to win its acceptance by the regions whose deputies had agreed to it. The whole history of the Estates General is a long complaint from the French monarchy, which asks for delegates whose assent will mean something. And never—or almost never—was the monarchy to gain such assurance. In France the effective decision belonged not to the Estates General, but to the provincial Estates, to the local assemblies; and this is so true that the Estates General, even though rather numerous, never formed a real political institution. . . .

The irregularity of their convocation, their geographical dispersion, the very number of their delegates prevented the creation of a tradition. There was no roll of the French assemblies, no clerks to keep records of them. One must look to the very end of the Middle Ages and the Estates General of 1484 to find a journal of these Estates—private in nature—which informs us of just what happened. Yet we have regularly, almost since its establishment, the rolls of the English parliament, where we find what was proposed and what was decided. . . .[5]

The English parliament and the French Estates General were institutions of almost identical origin. But the one developed in a small kingdom whose ruler saw his power contested; the other developed in a large kingdom where, by very definition and by tradition, the king could only be absolute.

Notes

1. See A. F. Pollard, *The Evolution of Parliament,* 2d ed. (London, 1926).—Ed.
2. "Court in council"—Ed.
3. Literally, "bad seizure."—Ed.
4. The text reads "1248" by mistake.—Ed.
5. The author goes on to distinguish between the binding statute made by the English king in parliament and the royal ordinance of France which could be made or changed by any king; and between the English baronage, united and national when threatened, and the French provincial nobilities, too numerous to assemble together, and in some cases, incapable of understanding each other.—Ed.

Part Five

IN SEARCH OF ORIGINS: RECENT EXPLANATIONS

Chapter 12 THE "CORPORATIST" VIEW OF PARLIAMENTARY ORIGINS

The historians who had most assiduously studied medieval assemblies generally found it difficult to explain them save in terms of their specific features and analogous antecedents. The alternative view that the comparative origins of representative institutions are better understood in broadly social and legal terms was not original with ÉMILE LOUSSE (b. 1905), but no other scholar has so lucidly and persuasively marshalled the evidence for it. Professor in the University of Louvain, Lousse presided over the International Commission for the History of Representative and Parliamentary Institutions for many years, influencing, editing and contributing to its many publications.

... The historiography of assemblies of Estates ... has been influenced by two great currents, one of which—older and hitherto stronger—has partly neutralized the favorable effect of the other. These currents proceed from two different conceptions of the subject: the parliamentary, or parliamentarist, conception held by the French or Anglo-French school, and the theory of the *Ständestaat,* which we prefer to call the corporatist conception, of the German school. The parliamentarist conception prevailed strongly as long as the prestige of contemporary parliamentarism remained uncontested. But as this prestige declined, it appeared more

From Émile Lousse, "Parlementarisme ou corporatisme? Les origines des assemblées d'états," *Revue Historique de Droit Français et Étranger,* 4e sér., IV (1935), 684-706 (abridged; footnotes omitted). Translated by editor. By permission of the author and of *Revue Historique de Droit français et Étranger.*

and more clearly that the corporatist, or corporative, approach alone provides a satisfying interpretation of the texts and the facts. . . .

The parliamentarist conception arose in the eighteenth century almost simultaneously in France and in England. . . .

But the dominant characteristics of the parliamentarist conception were most clearly evident in the monographs published by the École des Chartes at Paris, or under the influence of its masters in the course of the past fifty or sixty years. The "institutional" point of view prevailed: assemblies of Estates were studied not as an essential element in a very complicated political machinery, but as . . . an institution apart, that one should and even must isolate . . .the accent was put on the particularities of each assembly, although one might have thought it more interesting to relate it to others. Questions of public and administrative law were stressed at the expense of social or economic problems, or of private law and corporate discipline. . . . The problem of origins was dealt with as if there could not have been true assemblies before the first regular gatherings of the *three* orders. The vote of taxes is the principal competence of the institution, and one must reject as "false Estates" those assemblies convoked only to be consulted.

The adherents of the parliamentarist conception have accumulated . . . an imposing mass of materials; that is undoubtedly their greatest merit. But . . . the problem of the origins of the assemblies of Estates is not solved. . . .

The corporatist conception of the German school is a much more recent invention than the parliamentarist approach. It could hardly have attracted the Philosophes of the later eighteenth century, who saw in corporations of all sorts obstacles to the free expression of the individual. . . . It was morally incapable of triumphing in the nineteenth century in lands so individualist as France and England. . . .

It was the great German medievalists, liberals and convinced nationalists like F. C. Dahlmann, W. Wattenbach and G. Waitz, who seem to have been the first to advocate the historical study of the medieval *standische Verfassung*[1] in general; it was they who, forsaking special studies of the regional assembly, favored and encouraged the elaboration of the first theories of the *Ständestaat*, the embryos of corporative doctrines. . . .

The corporatist conception, as manifest in works of the German school, has produced remarkable results; but . . . until now, its sphere of application has been broadly limited to the lands of central Europe and to the schools influenced by the Germans. . . . The corporatists agree scarcely better than the parliamentarists on the question of the origins of assemblies of Estates. So it is perhaps not useless to specify the fundamental propositions of a doctrine which alone promises to lead to a satisfactory solution of the problem of the origins of the Estates in all of Christian Europe and also to a more exact acquaintance with the ideas, institutions and political constitutions of the Middle Ages and of modern times.

The first doctrinal proposition relates to the terminology: . . . it is a question of admitting . . . the use of the term "corporative state" to translate the German *Ständestaat*. The term "corporative state" is suggested naturally by the social, economic and political evolution of our time. It seems preferable to "corporative regime," which it is usual to apply more particularly to the economy. . . .

The corporative state of the Middle Ages is constituted in its essence by a triple hierarchy: territorial, administrative and political. As territorial hierarchy . . . , it appears, in its genesis and depending on the case, as one of the great fiefs formed from the dismemberment of the Carolingian Empire, as the agglomeration of several *pagi*[2] under one prince, lordships or principalities once practically independent of one another, even as a confederation of Estates or as a hybrid political form comparable to the confederation properly speaking. In the territory so constituted, the prince establishes progressively a hierarchy of functionaries, more and more complicated (*das Beamtentum*); the "territorial state" is also an "administrative state." And while the administrative hierarchy thus forms in complete dependence on a lord who tends to become a monarch, there arises on the other hand a political hierarchy of individuals, associations and orders (*das Standewesen*). The distinctions between the inhabitants of a given territorial state are based on the diversity of their social functions, of their economic conditions and of their legal and familial status; thus, one distinguishes between clerks, nobles, burghers and free peasants. Individuals of the same function, the same condition and the same private status are grouped in associations; and certain associations, endowed in turn with their own regulation, if not with full juridical personality, become privileged corporations: such are the abbeys, certain chapters, universities, fiefs, towns, franchises, rural communities, etc. At the highest level of the hierarchy are found one or several orders, or Estates, that is, one or more privileged groups of corporations of the same kind, which assume, in collaboration with the prince, the general direction of the affairs of the community.

The political organization of the corporative state is in unstable equilibrium; and we arrive at the theory of dualism, or of the duality of powers, generally admitted by German historians and jurists. The hierarchy of individuals, corporations and orders is acephalous. The prince, who heads the territorial and the administrative hierarchy, should normally dominate the former as well. At a given moment, he tries to master it: to assert his domination of the orders, he begins to convoke them around him to ask their "aid and counsel." But they, fortified with privileges granted for the most part by the prince or by his predecessors to individuals, to associations, to themselves and to the region as a whole, sometimes refuse to submit. This opposition of interests, of rights and powers, this struggle ends in compromise: by the creation of a regular and virtually permanent representation of the orders, not *under* the prince, as he would certainly have preferred, but *opposite* him (*die Standevertretung*). The representatives of the orders divide the supreme power with the prince, in the sense that their legitimate privileges stand in the way of his unlimited exercise of *potestas*.[3] This is not a "separation" of the different branches of a sovereignty still poorly defined, but a "division," a dualism, a duality of powers on the uniformly contractual basis of charters of all kinds. And at the moment when the representation of the orders is so organized, one can infer the existence of an assembly of Estates in a given territory.

This corporative form of state, provided with its triple hierarchy and based on more or less dualist sharing of powers, existed in all the countries of Christian Europe at the end of the Middle Ages and the beginning of modern times. We adopt Mr. Hintze's thesis,[4] under one or another of its aspects. Its negative aspect: the corporative state, as just defined, did not exist outside Christian Europe nor in epochs other than the close of the Middle Ages and in the centuries immediately following. Its positive aspect: this corporative state existed at this time in all the European and Christian peoples, everywhere broadly similar and differing only in accidental respects. . . .

There follow from the corporatist conception thus summarized . . . appreciable consequences for methods of research and of interpretation of the facts. We believe to have demonstrated that it is necessary to study the origins of an assembly of Estates less as the appearance of a new "institution" in a society otherwise unchanged, but rather as the culmination of a series of general transformations: as the completion of a "constitution," of a social, economic, juridical and political system born of slow gestation. The critical point is not to say just when and in what circumstances the assembly of Estates convened for the first time, but to define when the corporative state assumed its basic characteristics and replaced the tribal or feudal order. Once the existence of the corporative state has been determined, one can infer that of the assembly of orders, but it would be vain to attempt to establish the existence of the assembly without having first worked out the formation of the state. One should give up the practice of placing more or less conjectural considerations about the origins at the start of a monograph on the history of an assembly of Estates, and resolve to speak of that delicate question in the final chapter of a work relating to the formation of the corporative state. It is no less necessary to abandon the classical definition of the partisans of the parliamentarist theory, in favor of a larger and more comprehensive one, more genetic and more universal.[5]

In order to arrive at a certain conclusion for each particular case and, at the same time, to furnish duly ascertained materials for comparative study, one must carefully distinguish the essential from the accessory. . . . Such is the danger of strictly monographic work, elaborated according to rules formulated by the positivists. What is essential, in the formation of the corporative state and the genesis of an assembly of Estates, is the triple hierarchy of territory, administration and polity; the constitution and the representation of the associations and orders, the duality of powers. That is what is inherent in the very nature of the regime and is therefore found everywhere. What is accessory, accidental, is what varies according to circumstances of time and place, it is what differentiates the examples of concrete realization without prejudice to the unity and homogeneity of the system. Such are the name of the orders of their assembly, the date of their first regular and plenary convocation, the number of orders represented, the number of houses or courts which make up the assembly, the periodicity of sessions, the financial and fiscal competence and activity of the orders convoked by the prince[6] the constitutional form of the corporative state.

The comparative method serves not only to show identities but also to bring out differences. And institutions which manifest distinct accidental particularities are not necessarily different institutions.

As regards the knowledge of facts, the most notable consequence of the adoption of the corporatist point of view will undoubtedly be to hasten the solution of the problem, still open, of the origins of assemblies of Estates. The parliamentarist conception and prejudices will be jettisoned and the questions will be envisaged no longer in relation to modern parliamentary institutions, but in the way they were really posed at the end of the Middle Ages; it is not because the history of such and such a parliament presents no hiatus for five or six centuries that these assemblies were originally what they are today. Let us propose a general and coherent theory which will perfectly account for the unity of the political system in force in all Christian Europe at the dawn of the Renaissance. Thereby we shall find the family resemblance that existed between the old representative bodies. We shall clearly discern what differentiates the corporative state from the feudal state that preceded it and from the monarchy described as absolute which generally succeeded it. We shall provide a more faithful description of assemblies of Estates, seeing that the accessory will have been distinguished from the essential, and we shall naturally locate the characteristic traits of their organization on different planes. . . .

Notes

1. "Corporate constitution."—Ed.
2. The *pagus* was a territorial entity centering on the Roman city or a Germanic ethnic unity in the early Middle Ages.—Ed.
3. "Power."—Ed.
4. Lousse cites O. Hintze, "Weltgeschichtliche Bedingungen der Repräsentativverfassung," *Historische Zeitschrift*, CXLIII (1931), 21-39.
5. We propose the following definition: "An assembly of Estates is a political assembly, composed of representatives of the politically privileged order or orders of a country, acting in the name of these orders and of the country as a whole, to maintain, on the one hand, the privileges of the orders, associations and individuals, and, on the other hand, to render to the prince the services stipulated in the charters as the compensation for the rights and privileges granted by him."
6. The financial and fiscal competence of assemblies is a very important element to be sure,

but, on our view, not essential. It is because the "parliamentary" character of assemblies of Estates has been mistaken that the significance of their financial activity has been exaggerated. For us, this activity is simply a corollary of the dualism of powers. . . .

Chapter 13 MEDIEVAL REPRESENTATION A CONSEQUENCE OF THE REVIVAL OF ROMAN LAW

Possibly the most original contribution to the recent discussion of the rise of representative institutions is that of the American historian GAINES POST (b. 1902), emeritus professor of history at Princeton University. In a remarkable series of articles, collected under the title *Studies in Medieval Legal Thought: Public Law and the State, 1100-1322* (Princeton, 1964), Professor Post has argued that the revived Roman law contributed the concepts and devices requisite for representation as it came to be practiced in the later Middle Ages.

Mediaeval representation was constructed of heterogeneous materials on a foundation of feudal law, local institutions (hundred and county courts, guilds and corporations, communes, boroughs, and communities of villages), new classes in society (townsmen and knights of the shire), royal curias as assemblies, ecclesiastical synods and councils, and the growth of royal and papal authority. But in the course of construction the architects were greatly aided and stimulated by the revival of Roman and Canon Law, from which they obtained not only ideas but also the almost indispensable procedure of corporate representation by agents (*procuratores* or syndics) who were given full powers (*plena potestas*) by their constituents to represent the interests of the corporation in court. By granting such power of

From Gaines Post, "Roman Law and Early Representation in Spain and Italy, 1150-1250," *Speculum*, XVIII (1943), 211-224, 229-232 (abridged; footnotes omitted). Reprinted by permission of author and of The Medieval Academy of America.

attorney the corporation consented, before a civil suit began, to the jurisdiction of the judges and to their decision of the case. In the mandate which he carried the proctor was considered to be 'fully instructed' if *plena potestas* or its equivalent was stated; and the court generally demanded that the proctor have full powers. If the case 'touched' the legal rights of several defendants, the court could not give a just decision unless all had been properly cited—in accordance with the principle of due process and judicial consent clearly expressed by the classical jurist Paulus, 'De unoquoque negotio praesentibus omnibus, quos causa contingit, iudicari oportet,'[1] and, more sweepingly, by Justinian in the famous maxim, 'Quod omnes similiter tangit, ab omnibus comprobetur.[2] When a 'national emergency' involved the *status regni*,[3] it touched the interests and rights of all greater individuals and communities of lesser persons and corporations; and by the Roman principle of consent they must all be summoned to defend their property and other legal rights—the communities through their representatives bearing full powers to act in the name of their constituents and to accept the decision of the king's council and court in assembly. But this was made possible by the growing power of the king, who alone could declare a national emergency that must be met for the common good, the 'common utility', and whose prerogative, which consisted of the supreme 'law-finding,' judicial and administrative authority, but was limited by the law, enabled him to summon all whose rights were affected and who must respond to the summons or else be declared contumacious.[4]

This system of corporate representation by delegates given full powers flourished throughout western Europe by 1300—in provincial and general councils of the Church, in Parliament, in Cortes, and, slightly later, in States General. But when and where did it first develop? Priority has most frequently been awarded to Spain, where, it has long been said, as early as 1163 in Aragon, 1188 in Leon, the third estate was represented by *procuradores*. Ernest Barker, however, was inclined to give the credit for originality to the Dominican Order in the influence of its provincial and general chapters on the rise of Parliament.[5] But such claims for this or that priority have neglected the necessary presuppositions of the favorable environment, both of organized communities which had rights to defend and of the new law which provided a satisfactory means of representation.

1. THE LEGAL ENVIRONMENT

If up to about the middle of the twelfth century bare references are made in legal literature to proctors representing individuals, there is little mention of proctors or syndics of corporate communities other than churches. This is true of the early Bolognese and Provençal legists, and it is still true in Provence about 1149; at about the same time the early work of Rogerius reveals a discussion of proctors for individuals only, but his *Summa Codicis*[6] refers to the *yconomus* as acting for a church. From the middle of the century on, however, this literature greatly developed in Italy at Bologna, Modena, and Mantua, and in southern France at Montpellier (after 1162); and discussions of syndics and corporations began to appear in the works of the pupils and successors of the four great doctors of Bologna. In Italy Placentinus, who later was at Montpellier, *ca* 1166-83 and 1189-92, Pillius and Bencivenne were by the last quarter of the century briefly discussing the problem of the syndic as the oath-taker for a *collegium*. [7] Relatively full maturity among the legists was reached by Azo in his famous *Summa Codicis* (1209), who treats corporations and their representatives in greater detail than his predecessors. The influence of the Italians spread anew to southern France (Montpellier) about 1162 and after through Rogerius and Placentinus; and by 1149 through Vacarius, a pupil of Martinus, Roman Law arrived, but did not take full hold, in England. Perhaps Glanville could thus equate *responsales* (the later attorneys) with proctors.

Far more than that of the legists and glossators, the influence of the revived Canon Law, in Gratian and the decretists, in the decretals from Pope Eugenius III on and in the decretalists, and above all in the procedure in ecclesiastical courts, was bound soon to spread the ideas of Roman Law into northern France and England. In the so-called *Decretum* of Gratian (*ca* 1140) there are references to proctors, and churches are treated as corporations, but true corporate representatives these proctors are not—they are apparently prelates acting as agents of their churches. In the flourishing French school of decretists, however, at Paris, Rheims, and Amiens after 1160, one finds some striking passages on proctors as legal representatives of corporations. The *Ordo iudiciarius Bambergensis*[8] (probably written in France, *ca* 1182-85) not only discusses proctors of corporations but offers perhaps the earliest example of *plena potestas* in the mandate of the proctor. Still earlier, 1160-79, the *Rhetorica ecclesiastica*,[9] probably written in or near Rheims, mentions in a form of appeal two syndics of the canons of a church.

Through the decretists, then, some knowledge of the Roman Law on the subject began to spread in ecclesiastical circles. But it was the papacy in the twelfth century that decisively started the practical application of Roman principles to the procedure in the courts of the Church. Pope Eugenius III (1145-53), a contemporary of Gratian, and a friend of Roman law and lawyers (so St. Bernard, with much scolding!), decided that the abbot and monks of Clairvaux should not be compelled to take the *iuramentum calumniae*[10] in court (such an oath was contrary to the monastic ideal, of course) but, 'sicut imperiales leges consentiunt,'[11] they should have an *oeconomus,* who could litigate and take the oath for them. The *oeconomus* is simply a business agent, but there is a close approach to the idea that a proctor should act for the corporation. In any event, the decretal shows how greatly the revived Roman Law was influencing the developing canon law. By the time of Clement III (1187-91) and Innocent III (1198-1216) ecclesiastical corporations with proctors (not the bishop or abbot as *ex officio procurator* of the church) were clearly recognized in the practice of the Roman Curia, and the decretalists became increasingly active in defining and refining the terminology to be used for corporations and their agents in lawsuits.

The last third of the twelfth century, then, is the period when the literature on corporations and their representatives in the courts began to flourish. Both legists and canonists were trying to adapt the Roman procedure to the courts of secular and ecclesiastical lords. But the practical acceptance of their new methods was no doubt slow. In Italy, little evidence appears of elected proctors or syndics of municipalities or city councils until the last two decades of the twelfth century, although consuls and *judices*,[12] as administrative officers, may earlier have been a practical equivalent. In France the secular courts may have tried lawsuits of corporate representatives fairly early, but not long before the beginning of the thirteenth century. In England, only in the ecclesiastical courts should we expect the common practice (Glanville's *responsales* were not discussed as corporate agents), but Henry II's courts had experience in summoning proctors of a monastery. In all Spain there seems to have been no real school of law before the thirteenth century; Spanish ecclesiastics are not found as legists or canonists until the latter half of the twelfth century, and very few then; but practical knowledge of the procedure must have existed in church courts. Moreover, some influence of the Roman Law taught at Montpellier and Bologna spread at least into the County of Barcelona (the relations of Provence and Genoa and Pisa with the County were close, as is well known), but it was tenuous until the thirteenth century; and no evidence has yet appeared that any practical use of corporate procuration was made in the secular courts of Spain before the thirteenth century. Yet before 1200 some experience in handling corporate representatives must have been gained both from local prelates, whose affairs were often treated in secular courts and who sometimes served as judges in the royal *curia*, and from Italian merchants.

Actually the history of the new procedure is yet to be written. But it seems possible to conclude that the practice of corporate representation hardly began before about 1150—and not significantly, except in the Church, until the last quarter of the century even in Italy. It is as if the lawyers and judges had suddenly realized that there were numerous communes with their institutions and officers, and numerous merchant and craft guilds, and that they must at once apply the newly discovered principles of the Roman law to them. Once more the rise of Bologna and the new Roman Law are of the utmost importance in the civilization of the twelfth century. The Roman Law and the lawyers, however, had first to overcome the feudal and Germanic law, in which it was difficult for any but the principal parties, or the administrators in communities, to appear in court. The process was slower, no doubt, in Spain, northern France, England and Germany, than in Italy. If the appointment of corporate agents for lawsuits lagged behind the theory—the appearance of city magistrates or prelates in the courts to plead for their communities or churches was the old practice, and it long continued with the new—how far behind lagged the practice of summoning to royal assemblies proctors and syndics with mandates from the towns?

2. EARLY REPRESENTATION IN SPAIN

Despite the lack of definite evidence of any practical application of the principles of corporate representation in Spanish courts, it has time and again been either implied or directly asserted that the third estate was represented by *procuradores* in the Cortes of the Spanish kingdoms by the end of the twelfth century. It is quite true, of course, that citizens of members or the city councils (*concejos*) were occasionally summoned. But were they corporate representatives, empowered by mandates to carry the will of their communities to the king in his council, or simply local magistrates and prominent members of the *concejos* who had information on local custom and law, took oaths of fealty to the king in his high court, and received the royal commands issued by the king's council and court of prelates and magnates? Records of the Cortes of Leon and Castile reveal the presence of *cives electi* (Leon, 1188),[13] 'many from each city' (Benevente, 1202), 'a multitude of citizens sent by the cities' (Leon, 1208), or 'good men' (Seville, 1252; Valladolid, 1258; Toledo, 1260). By 1269, however, there may have been true *procuradores*, for 'los de los concejos de las cuidades y villas' appeared at Burgos, although it is not until 1305 that the term *procurador de concejo* is actually used. We therefore have no clear evidence of corporate, proctorial representation until 1305.

Even earlier than in the Kingdom of Leon, according to the generally accepted account, *procuradores* of cities regularly were summoned to the Cortes of Aragon, notably at Saragossa, 1163 or 1164. . . . To the assembly itself, a feudal *curia*, the king had summoned for counsel prelates, barons and the cities; and in the assembly oaths of fealty and obedience to the *constitutio*[14] were taken by all those present. Here it is that the document is of vital interest: it gives the names of sixteen 'adelantados de concilio Cesarauguste'[15] as taking the oath 'asensu et voluntate et mandamento tocius concilii,'[16] seven 'adelantados de concilio de Darocha,' five 'adelantados de concilio de Oscha,' some eight *adelantados* from another city, and about twenty 'alfaches de Uno Castello.'[17]

In this remarkable document no use of the term *procurador* appears. But the *adelantados de concejo* of Saragossa and the other cities, were they not representatives sent by the municipal *concejo*, and consequently the same in function as the *procuradores* of the thirteenth century? To be sure they were representatives of the municipalities, but they were so numerous from each city that they bear only a faint resemblance to the proctors or syndics of Roman and Canon Law. The term *adelantados* itself seems in this instance to mean simply members of the *concejo*, or magistrates at the same time, like the Italian consuls and judges. Again it is possible that taken literally the word indicates not merely members but members sent out in the place of the whole *concejo*. Here might be an approach to thirteenth-century proctors or syndics, for these sometimes were sent in Italy and France in fairly large numbers, and, significantly, the *adelantados* took the oath 'asensu et voluntate et mandamento tocius concilii Cesarauguste.' Nevertheless, if the feeling of community is revealed, such informal representation was hardly corporate in the legal sense of Roman and Canon Law in the later twelfth and thirteenth centuries. . . .

After 1163 the next Cortes noted for the representation of the cities was that of Lérida, 1214. Now this Cortes seems to have been also a legatine council, composed of both clergy and laity, for over it presided the Cardinal-Legate Peter of Benevento, by mandate of Innocent III (Pedro II had been a vassal of the pope). It resulted in a *constitucio pacis et treuge*[18] promulgated by the papal legate in the name of the pope and of King James I, and with the 'acclaim' of the bishops and other prelates of Aragon and Catalonia, and of many magnates 'et plurium aliorum.'[19] In the *constitutio* itself, really a *Landfried*[20] in character, no doubt intended to establish law and order immediately after the tragic defeat and death of Pedro II at Muret, the Cardinal-Legate Peter speaks merely of having the *consilium* of the prelates 'et aliorum prudencium virorum.'[21] But it is certainly significant that the peace and truce proclaimed must be sworn to by the nobility, knights, *cives* and *burgenses castrorum et villarum;*[22] further, that the *cives et populi* of each *civitas*, with the advice of the bishop, were to elect two *paciarii*,[23] one 'de majoribus'[24] and one 'de populo,'[25] who with the vicar chosen from each city by the *Procurator* of Catalonia should take public oath to observe the peace and maintain the provisions of the *constitutio;* and that all the *cives* of cities and the *homines of loci*[26] should take the same oath. Finally, there is even a provision (cap. 20) against any extraordinary financial imposition by the king on the cities, which hints at some resistance put up by the city representatives.

Were these representatives *procuradores?* The *Chronicle* of James I of Aragon tells us that the royal council summoned to Lérida ten men from each city, who were to be 'furnished with powers from the rest to approve that which might be done by all' (the Roman formula that was the legal equivalent of *plena potestas*), and that all those present took an oath of fealty to the king. Such a delegation of ten furnished with powers would so strongly resemble proctors or syndics that one might well conclude at once that the meeting of the Cortes of 1214 is the earliest known example of proctorial representation in Aragon and Catalonia—indeed, in all Spain. Unfortunately, since the *Chronicle* of James I—he was only six years old in 1214—was written much later, and possibly not by the king himself, we cannot be sure that conditions in the latter half of the century are not reflected here. Nevertheless, there may have been corporate representation, because the papal legate, perhaps aware of the precedent set by Innocent III in summoning mandataries of Italian cities to the Curia, may have intentionally instructed the cities of Aragon to send true proctors. It is significant, certainly, that the cities were already protesting through representatives against extraordinary subsidies. If proctors were thereafter appointed as representatives in Catalonia and Aragon in the thirteenth century, there is no specific mention of them: it is *cives*, simply, who are indicated as attending *Cortes*. But in 1283 the two to four representatives of each town were probably real proctors.

What kind of representation this was in twelfth and early thirteenth-century Spain can be understood only through a thorough knowledge of town government in relation to the kings. No real history of the rising Spanish communes and informally organized towns has been written. At the moment, therefore, we can only point to the problem by stating it. By the middle twelfth century some organized towns, recognized by the kings of Leon and Castile and of Aragon, had *concejos* which were composed usually of the more prominent citizens and property owners. Probably the magistrates, *alcaldes* and *merinos*, or judges, and others, were sometimes elected 'popularly' or in the *concejo;* but the town institutions are so poorly known that we cannot be sure when the magistrates were locally elected and when chosen by a local lord or by the king himself. If business or lawsuits involved a town, it is likely that the magistrates and a group of leading councillors or citizens personally negotiated the affair or went to court; there are no signs of any mandate issued to agents, who were not at the same time magistrates, to conclude the business or accept the judges' sentence. In the twelfth century an older, informal, representation was customary: it was individualistic rather than corporate; for if a vague conception of the corporate vassal—with the commune as the vassal—existed in Italy and Spain, in practice it was the individual, prominent citizens who were responsible, not a corporate person. . . . Since in twelfth-century Spain there was little if any conscious theory of corporate communities, whatever the practical development of communes, there was no suitable machinery of representation. This situation has been observed, and it is reflected in the diversity of language used in the documents to mention the presence of townsmen in the Cortes. A rough and ready system of informal representation, however, was possibly adopted for the summons to the Cortes of Leon and Castile, 1188-1208, and of Aragon, 1163-1214. For example, the *Fuero*[27] granted to Toledo (1118; confirmed in 1176) provided that 'decem ex maioribus civitatis,'[28] who were probably the local judges, should come to the king to give him information about violations of the royal privilege: we may suppose that if similar institutions flourished in other towns, the *cives electi* at Leon in 1188 and in later Cortes of Leon and Castile were sometimes groups of ten or more summoned to give information to the king and thus help him and his councillors (the prelates and magnates) decide how to formulate the provisions of *constitutiones* for law and order. . . .

What seems to be certain, however, is that representation of a really corporate kind (in which the agents were responsible to their constituents, even though they must obey a superior jurisdiction in the king's court and council) did not arise as a system in Spain before the second half of the thirteenth century—with the possible exception of the Cortes of Lérida in 1214— either because the influence of the Romano-canonical procedure was not yet sufficiently felt, or because the kings were not yet powerful enough to make a logical system of centralization and local, corporate and individual rights work effectively. But representation of a loose kind there was—as early as the middle of the twelfth century. The moment towns were granted royal charters and rights of organization, they assumed enough prestige and responsibility to be summoned to the feudal *curia* of the king; and members of town councils, usually as judges and magistrates, carried the 'record,' or information on local conditions of law and justice, to the feudal assembly, took oaths of fealty to the king, and were placed under the obligation of returning home to carry out the decisions of the king and his magnates. The delegates were representatives of the king in the cities. They did not participate directly in the council and court of magnates and prelates who gave counsel and consent and judged important cases; their consent, if any, was not 'popular,' but rather the consent involved in defending local rights based on custom and royal franchise. The early Spanish Cortes, then, was still a feudal assembly in which the decisions of matters of law and justice, taxation, and treaties were made by the king and his *curia*. . . .

3. ITALY

In the twelfth century, Italian assemblies, like those in Spain, already were attended by delegates from the towns; but these delegates were, again like those in Spain, chiefly legal experts and local magistrates who brought the record to the royal authority, took oaths of fealty to the king, and to all intents and purposes represented rather the power of the king in the communities than the interests and rights of their fellow citizens. Pope Innocent III,[29] however, summoned *procuratores* with full power from six cities of the March of Ancona to meet with his Curia. If we cannot be sure that no true proctors had been sent to assemblies in the earlier period, it is at least not surprising that the papal chancery of Innocent III was fully acquainted with the Roman terminology and meaning of corporate representation. In the pope's letter of 1200, addressed to the *potestas*[30] and *populus* of each of the cities, we learn that a papal legate, sent to establish order in the March of Ancona, had been instructed to order the cities, after common deliberation, to send to the Curia. . . . *procuratores and nuntii*[31] [who] were to have full power from their constituents . . . to appear at the Curia and receive the papal commands for establishing law and order, and to swear fealty, so that their communes could not later refuse obedience to the pope on the pretense that they had not sanctioned what the proctors might engage them to do. And they were also to give counsel to the pope, counsel which no doubt consisted largely of the record of local exemptions or franchises, of cases of lawlessness, of matters pertaining to the municipal administration, and of petitions to the pope. . . .

This representation was feudal in nature. But it was something more than feudal, for it signalled the new emphasis upon the central authority, which was enhanced by the Roman corporate terminology and machinery of representation now maturely developed by Innocent III and his Curia. The essential terminology at least (the number of representatives from each city had to be fixed later) differed little from that used a century later by Edward I in his summons to Parliament. As in the case of earlier imperial and Spanish assemblies, however, there is no likelihood that the representatives of the third estate did more than give information, petition, and receive decisions. As for the consuls and *podestàs* as proctors, they were chosen because they were local judges and administrators, hence, if the ruler could assert his authority, really representatives of pope or prince in the cities. Nevertheless, the fact that they brought powers from their constituents was a long step forward in the development of a system of corporate representation; thereby some responsibility for defending, in the ruler's court and assembly, the rights of their communities was already imposed upon the delegates.

5. CONCLUSIONS

After the first decade of the thirteenth century the system of corporate representation by agents given full powers grew steadily. By broadening the legal experience of Italian communes and accepting the formulas and procedure developed by legists and canonists Pope Innocent III played an important if not original and decisive rôle in the adoption of the new method of representing communities in ecclesiastical and secular assemblies. He was the first pope to summon proctors to represent cathedral chapters and convents in a Universal Council (Fourth Lateran, 1215), and his legate in Catalonia perhaps instructed delegates of the cities to bring mandates to the Cortes of Lérida (1214). It is surely no accident that under the immediate successors of Innocent III the Dominican Order adopted a system of general chapters which, although it owed much to the experience of the monastic orders of the twelfth century, also owed to Roman and canon law the idea of the representation of provinces (groups of convents) by priors and *diffinitores* who were given full powers. Nor can it be entirely an accident that the first secular ruler definitely known to have summoned proctors with mandates or powers was Frederick II. After the middle of the century the procedure of proctorial representation continued in the Kingdom of Sicily and in the Papal States, and definitely took hold in Spain, England and France. By 1268 Roman formulas of the proctorial mandate were adapted for the use of knights of the shire in Parliament; and soon the kings of England and France, following the precedent established by the lawyers and by cathedral chapters in provincial councils, began to express the Roman principle of due process in court, 'Quod omnes tangit, etc." as an integral part of the *rationale* of the representation of individual and corporate rights before the king and his court and council in assembly.

The paucity and vagueness of the sources for the early period of representation (1150-1250) permit no final conclusions either on the kind of consent which the delegates brought to the assembly or on the real meaning attached to the new formulas in the various countries. The legal thought involved in the new style of representation cannot therefore be defined with confidence, although it seems to have been approaching a logical application by 1250. But it is at least safe to conclude that corporate representation appeared in Italy earlier than in Spain, and that, whether it was magistrates or true corporate agents who came to the assemblies, there was no conception of popular, or sovereign, consent; if the interests of the communities were defended, nonetheless early representation was more that of the ruler in the towns than that of the towns in the royal *curia* and assembly.

Notes

1. "It is fitting for any business to be judged in the presence of all to whom the cause pertains."–Ed.
2. "What touches all alike should be approved by all."–Ed.
3. "State (or condition) of the realm."–Ed.
4. See below, Document J.1, p. 147.–Ed.
5. Post cites Barker's *The Dominican Order and Convocation* (Oxford, 1913), observing that Barker's thesis has never attracted much approval."–Ed.
6. A commentary on the *Code* (of Justinian).–Ed.
7. "College," i.e., a form of corporation.–Ed.
8. This title may be translated as the "Bamberg treatise on court procedure."–Ed.
9. "Ecclesiastical Rhetoric"–Ed.
10. "Oath of calumny."–Ed.
11. "In accordance with imperial laws."–Ed.
12. "Judges"–Ed.
13. "Elected citizens"; excerpts from the record of this assembly are printed as Document D, p. 143.–Ed.
14. "Constitution," the official record of the assembly.–Ed.
15. "Leading men of the community of Zaragoza."–Ed.
16. "By the assent and will and order of the whole community.–Ed.
17. The towns mentioned are Daroca, Huesca, and Uncastillo, all in Aragon.–Ed.
18. "Constitution of the peace and truce" (of God).–Ed.
19. "And of many others."–Ed.
20. "Peace of the land," a kind of territorial order sometimes derived from the peace of God and distinct from the law of fiefs or of vassals.–Ed.
21. "And of other prudent men."–Ed.
22. "Citizens (and) burghers of castles and towns."–Ed.
23. "Peace-men"–Ed.
24. "Of the great men."–Ed.
25. "Of the lesser people."–Ed.
26. "Men (of) places"–Ed.
27. The *fuero* was a statement, or charter, of custom.–Ed.
28. "Ten of the greater [men] of the city."–Ed.
29. 1198-1216.–Ed.
30. *Podestà*: i.e., the special administrator of an Italian town.–Ed.
31. "Messengers."–Ed.

Chapter 14 FROM PRE-PARLIAMENT TO PARLIAMENT

In what Professor Lousse calls the "parliamentarist" school, there was unanimity that assemblies of Estates were not to be confused with the primitive consultative bodies that antedated them. But little attention (after an unenlightening debate in late nineteenth-century France) was devoted to the characteristics of the early assemblies and the process of their transformation. ANTONIO MARONGIU (b. 1902), Professor of the History of Political Institutions at the University of Rome and since 1970 President of the International Commission for the History of Representative and Parliamentary Institutions, renews the question of the parliamentary origins of privileged assemblies in a comparative study of medieval parliaments which was first published in 1949 in conjunction with a monograph on Italian representative institutions.

As we have seen, solemn reunions of secular and ecclesiastical dignitaries were summoned by sovereigns whenever it seemed opportune to ask their counsel or opinion. They were also used to publicise among the king's subjects special events, such as new legislative or judicial measures, international treaties, or dynastic marriages. These assemblies were nearly always events of great importance in the history of their countries. But our information about them is extremely fragmentary, making it difficult to delineate their character and traits with any precision. According to some historians, however, it is possible to differentiate and distinguish two separate types of meetings.

The assemblies were widespread. They varied in importance and at some stage acquired a definite role as an institution related to the practice of government in

From Antonio Marongiu, *Medieval Parliaments: A Comparative Study*, tr. S. J. Woolf (London: Eyre and Spottiswoode, 1968), pp. 45-57. Reprinted by permission of the author.

the different countries. Some of the members of these assemblies—because of what they represented in the country—possessed an exceptional position and function which cannot be ignored. At a certain point, varying from country to country, these great assemblies ceased to represent purely isolated moments in the history of the country. They developed with increasing clarity, authority and awareness into institutions distinctly related to each other by something more than mere chronological succession or the arbitrary caprice of sovereigns. At this point a new type or category of assembly had emerged which superseded and substituted, without abolishing, the old type of assembly.

In practice, the earlier assemblies were political manifestations called to give solemnity to dynastic events, such as the accession of a new sovereign, the promulgation of laws of the solemn publication of treaties. But alongside these, other more frequent assemblies were convoked by sovereigns to obtain the counsel of particularly qualified or authoritative subjects and to ask them for assistance. They were consultative assemblies, but when unanimous they could accept or grant like deliberative bodies. Then, as if by natural evolution, most of the members of the earlier assemblies seemed to disappear, and the assemblies acquired a new logical form, a new spirit, dimension and political significance. Their external formal structure remained similar to that of the preceding consultative and executive assemblies. Indeed, the division and organization of these assemblies or parliaments into "chambers," "houses," *bracci, stati* or *stamenti* came quite late and was dependent on a formal institutional grouping of the three main social categories. It was a purely structural phenomenon which, once fully established, gave many of the medieval and post-medieval representative institutions the appearance and name of "assemblies of estates," or simply "estates," *stati, stamenti, Stände,* etc. But the true novelty, the new unitary, psychological, teleological dimension, is to be found in the self-consciousness of the approach towards public affairs of those most concerned—the sovereign, members of the assembly and the country itself. This development is to be found before any formal changes.

These assemblies embodied a new institutional, representative situation and became a power in the state. Their members acted in a legally coherent and politically responsible manner, as constitutive elements expressing the will of a greater common body—the community. The self-conscious awareness of this new thing was an essential moment of the transformation. The assemblies developed from the earlier ones and did not contradict the system of consultations with the most important subjects. But it was no automatic or logical development.

Once the new institution had arisen, it tended to act as an institutional link between the king and his subjects, while its members acted as personal links between all the subjects and the general representative body. By now this assembly or parliamentary institution was an important element in the organisation of the state. Its convocation and sessions assumed an entirely different value from those of the old assemblies: it signified the recognition and exercise of the principle of representation, combined with those of collaboration and consent.

This seems to me the manner in which the older great assemblies evolved into a new pattern, containing genuine elements of the medieval parliament. Despite the fragmentary nature of the evidence, it seems possible to distinguish three distinct categories: (*a*) "public relations" assemblies, called to give solemnity to certain events; (*b*) great consultative assemblies, which often expressed consent by votes or acclamation, but which—lacking any collegial unity—possessed no deliberative powers; (*c*) a more complex and complete version of the latter, which as a body was juridically representative of the will of the country (or at least of the social groups organised within the country), and which through its deliberative powers acted, and was recognised, as a fundamental element in the structure of the state.

There seem to have been two distinct phases, each with its own concepts and structures. We should describe these as forerunners of parliament or pre-parliaments, and parliaments. The distinction is not original. For a long time historians have regarded the *cortes* of León of 1188[1] as different in character from the traditional great assemblies of the same period and even of the following period. What had appeared to be a normal meeting of ecclesiastical and lay dignitaries, called arbitrarily by the king for his own purposes, in order that its members might listen and acclaim and perhaps express personal opinions and points of view binding only on themselves, had been transformed into a new political and legal entity, reflecting a new order of social relations, political and administrative activities, etc.

But historians now seem more ready to move from this isolated case and accept the distinction as a valid criterion for comparative and analytical purposes. In England, Plucknett has differentiated between prototypes of parliaments and true parliaments. Spanish historians have distinguished *de facto cortes* from *de jure cortes*, limited curias (*curia reducida*) from the *curia plena*. Even French historians have expressed doubts about what character to attribute to the first great national assemblies—traditionally considered "estates general"—held under Philip the Fair and his immediate successors.

The new term "parliament" (*parlamentum, parlement,* etc.) was used as a synonum of *colloquium*. From this concept of a "conversation" or "discourse" between two or more persons it became synonymous with *conventus, curia, concio, etc.* In French the term was already to be found in the *Chanson de Roland* in the late 11th and early 12th century. In Latin it is first found in a papal document of Urban II of 1089, and then in the *Annali genovesi* of the chronicler Caffaro for 1101. In another papal document of 1107-10 it is to be found in a list of the feudal obligations of the inhabitants of Ninfa, where it is understood as a review of the feudal or citizen military contingents. Soon after, the chronicler Otto Morena used it to describe one of the diets of Roncaglia held by Frederick Barbarossa. It was frequently employed to describe similar events in France and England as well. In

Italy it was a common term to describe the popular assemblies of the communes (*parlamento, concione, colloquio*).

These communal popular assemblies fall outside the scope of our study. For we have restricted ourselves to representative and deliberative assemblies of large territorial areas such as states or provinces, as only these exemplify the concept we have given the term: the exclusion of any direct and immediate participation by the inhabitants in the government because of the size of the territory, and hence the need of forms of representation. . . .

The term "parliament" is undoubtedly ambiguous, as it described such diverse assemblies and changed in significance in different periods. Indeed, many writers prefer to speak of the history of "estates," of *assemblées d'états*, rather than of the history of parliaments. In fact, in continental Europe since the 15th century (in France, the Netherlands, Germany, Scandinavia, and even Savoy, Piedmont, Navarre and Sardinia) representative institutions were spoken of as *états, stati, stamenti*. Nevertheless, the term parliament seems more correct, as assemblies of "estates" were only a species of the genus parliament, defined according to their internal structure. It is clearly important to know whether a parliamentary institution consisted of one, two or three chambers—because of the effect this had on its procedure and activities. But all parliamentary institutions possessed basically similar functions. Moreover, the presence of "estates"—differentiated elements of society, true social bodies which developed common personalities and public functions of great importance from the 14th century onwards—seems to be neither original nor general (and consequently not essential) to parliaments. In France, Spain, Sicily, Flanders and elsewhere the division into estates within the great parliamentary assemblies arose later than the first assemblies. At first the participants spoke and acted purely as individual members of a single assembly. Only subsequently did they begin to speak and vote as members, not of parliament but of their respective *stato* or *braccio*. . . .

From the large body of literature on the definition of parliaments it is worth our while to pause and examine the contributions of Cadier, Lord[2] and Lousse. Cadier concentrated on the differences between the earlier irregular great assemblies, when the sovereign summoned his vassals to witness an important act, and later *assemblées d'états* in which the three orders had achieved their participation in the government and administration of the country. He was concerned with "provincial estates," but his observations can be applied to "estates general". He placed much emphasis on the regularity of the meetings. Undoubtedly the timing, customary nature and regularity of convocations are important elements to distinguish parliamentary institutions with a continuous life and functions of their own from sporadic, casual reunions, however solemn, which remained extraneous to the organisation of the state. Nevertheless, the regularity of reunions, while important, is merely indicative of the institutional nature of the assemblies, and is not an essential element. Indeed Cadier failed to take into account the representative character of these institutions and the functions and general implications of representation.

Lord also emphasised the regularity of meetings and the fixed forms of representation, but for him the decisive step in the transformation of the old feudal assemblies into something which could be considered representative of the entire population was the participation of the "third estate". This participation was undoubtedly important and reflected the development and growing influence of the cities and towns. But it was not, as Lord supposed, sufficient by itself to transform state or provincial assemblies from *de facto* bodies into institutions, from consultative into deliberative assemblies, or to give them a unity and personality, a common will, new and precisely defined attributes.

Lousse's definition remains the most persuasive. The *assemblée d'états* was "a political assembly composed of the representatives of the politically privileged order or orders of a country, who act in the name of these orders and of all the country, on the one hand to watch over the maintenance of the privileges of the orders, groups and individuals and the conservation of the fundamental rights of the country, and on the other hand to offer the prince the counterpart of the rights and privileges recognised and conceded by him". With this definition Lousse underlines the close relationship between the assemblies, the corporative organisation of medieval society and the representative and deliberative functions of the assembly. By defining the assembly as political, he agrees that the organ cannot be purely consultative. He denies that the number of orders is a determinant element, and emphasises that the parliament was representative not merely of this or that group, but of the community.

The weakness of his definition is its excessively comprehensive character. It is too broad to distinguish between the type of assembly he is interested in and the earlier medieval assemblies. His definition applies equally to assemblies of estates which met occasionally, sporadically, without continuity, and to those which possessed a legal continuity by virtue of their permanent insertion in the state structure as an intermediate organ between government and governed. Moreover, Lousse's definition would seem to be based on the idea of representation chosen "from below" (rather than nominated "from above") and in consequence over-emphasises the position . . . of subjects. . . .

The fundamental criterion for differentiating the varying types of *colloquia, tractatus, parlamenta, curiae, concilia*, etc., in the 12th century and later is, according to us, whether or not they were institutional bodies of political and legal importance and constitutional character. The way to ascertain this is to study whether they were of occasional or permanent character, the degree of their autonomy, their legal status, and the extent of their attributes and powers. Once these have been established, the nature of the assemblies—pre-parliaments or parliaments—can be determined.

The transformation of traditional medieval assemblies into parliaments did not occur everywhere, nor was it complete and definitive, nor did it occur at any specific moment. Above all, it meant a change of attitudes, a transformation of the will and determination of the members of the old assemblies. Hence it was frequently determined or facilitated by contingent factors, and often achieved only temporary results. In short, the transformation was slow, by no means always continuous, nor complete.

At the risk of over-simplification, we would suggest that this process occurred in one of the following ways:

1. The pre-parliamentary assembly of great feudal nobles (whatever its official title) became aware of itself as an organic whole, with a capacity and power of initiating and decision-making. As it acquired self-confidence, it developed and surpassed the limits originally placed on the activities and prerogatives of its members, and increasingly usurped power and initiatives without any previous agreement with the sovereign.

2. Through incapacity, weakness or even broadmindedness, or through inability to achieve a given end on his own, at a certain moment the king decided to consider the members of the assembly as embodying the community of which they were leaders. He decided to ask them for aid not as individuals, but also on behalf of those magnates who were absent, and indeed on behalf of the whole community. In this way he implicitly recognised in, or attributed to, the assembly the functions and powers of representation and decision.

3. Political groups in the country organised in leagues or unions, swore to act together and showed their strength in informal gatherings. They rose in arms and forced the sovereign not only to grant their petitions and complaints, but to accept that an assembly which represented either them or the "estates" of the country should participate in deciding major political questions as a matter of course. What the victors considered a triumph was, in purely legal terms, merely a concession. But once it had been achieved it formed a precedent, and by its continuation and repetition became obligatory and normal.

4. A parliamentary institution was created by imitation of analogous institutions in other countries, or as the specific result of international agreements. In fact, even if one leaves aside examples of territorial conquests or changes of dynasties...one must take account of the reciprocal influences and similarities of institutional developments in neighbouring countries or at analogous levels of civilisation or community life. In western Europe state boundaries never created an effective barrier against the spread of doctrines, of moral, legal, social or political beliefs.

Once these parliaments or "estates" were born and recognised as exercising their own distinct activities and powers within the structure of the state, they had reached the half-way mark of their evolution. They possessed and exercised representative functions for the most part as the result of an explicit legal decision and not through popular election. This was reflected in the nature of their relations with the sovereign and in the normally antithetical (but not hostile) position they assumed towards the organs of government. The consequences were a long and varied series of contractual agreements between the "realm" (or the people), personified by the assembly, and the king, holder of supreme power. These agreements normally included a grant of money by parliament, binding not only on its own members but on the whole country, in return for the sovereign's pledge to sanction and observe regulations and measures which possessed the force of law or statutes. The laws were thus irrevocable and could only be modified by a new agreement between the contracting parties.

The assemblies represented and deliberated. Within the limits imposed by the authority of sovereign and government, they expressed the participation of the "people" or "country" in the direction of public affairs, either by taking the initiative or by subsequent control. What an assembly stated or approved seemed to have been approved by all the people through the collaboration of the whole community. In this sense it could be said that the people had found the method and instrument of making their contribution to the government of public affairs.

This development could be seen not only when the parliament consisted of a single assembly, but when it was formed of "chambers," "estates," *stamenti, bracci, membri* or the like. In this latter case, the transformation of a *de facto* organisation into a new body expressing and realising a collective will took place at a double or multiple level. The various estates of each multiple parliament expressed themselves not as separate single parliaments, but as groups, each of which underwent the same process of unification we have considered in relation to the overall parliamentary body. This phenomenon of the consolidation and realisation of a collective will by the estates, the clergy, the higher and lower nobility, etc., merits further research, because it ran parallel, and was frequently related to the rise and early consolidation of parliamentary institutions themselves: sometimes indeed it was identical to them. For the most part one can explain this pattern of organisation in terms of the communal spirit of the medieval world. Wherever it occurred, the sovereign found himself confronted not by individuals, but by groups and bodies. In consequence, the structure of the new parliaments frequently emerged in the form of assemblies of "estates".

The new parliamentary institutions were without any solid doctrinal basis. They had arisen out of practical attempts to enlarge on the area of consent and collaboration in the government of public affairs of political and social forces. Hence it was never a question of achieving the best possible organisation of government and state, but rather of searching for immediate results which would gain most approval from those interested in their realisation and who were, in fact, obliged to bear the cost.

The path had been prepared by the tradition of fairly regular convocations of great assemblies, which made possible a dialogue between sovereign and people. But ultimately it had also been prepared by the Germanic concept of the king as head and leader of his people, and the medieval ideal of a king who did not commit, but who avoided abuses. The assemblies were an inherent part and consequence of the feudal order, for the king needed the counsel and aid of his vassals. Thus where parliaments were born they consisted of feudatories. The most suitable place for royal requests of counsel and aid was the parliamentary assembly. Moreover, parliament presented distinct advantages as an instrument of government, especially at difficult moments. By the meeting of assemblies, the sovereigns and their governments were able to keep in contact with the main currents of public opinion. They could seek to direct them towards their own objectives and bring to their notice certain facts (or the official version of such facts) and so influence them and encourage sentiments of loyalty among widespread social groups throughout their territories. At the same time, because parliament possessed representative responsibilities, it could be asked to supply soldiers and financial means. For until the later 15th or 16th century, the king had as little power to impose military service or arbitrary taxation on his subjects—and especially on his vassals—as the vassals had over their own dependants.

Thus parliamentary institutions were no more created out of a void than were fiefs and the feudal system. The conditions which gave birth to them could have lasted without change much longer, if human actions had not overcome the deadweight of inertia. No conscious choice was made to create either feudalism or parliamentary institutions. They developed out of the actions of inevitably only a small number of people. For the dialogue could only take place between the sovereign and subjects with a legal, economic or social status of such importance that the sovereign could not ignore them. In fact, the sovereigns sought for their loyalty, friendship and collaboration. Sovereigns had a right to ask counsel and aid of their vassals. But it was the king who chose his vassals and gave them their place in the feudal order.

In the corporative and feudal society of the Middle Ages, everyone was subject to precise limitations: royal vassals could not mobilise their dependants until they had shown that such an act corresponded to their own "privileges" and did not harm those of others. But what no individual vassal could do, parliament was able to, through the fiction that it represented the entire country including those who were not represented in or summoned to the assembly. In a sense, the new institutions filled a gap and gave reality to the terms "country," "land," "patria," "people," "kingdom," "the community of the subjects," which hitherto had existed as mere abstractions or figures of speech. Through parliament these abstractions came to life, and by their vote gave royal decisions unlimited authority and the moral support of "consent".

But parliament represented even more. The community felt itself united in the recognition of its general and common interests, and in the formation and coordination of the interests of its separate parts, each of which had acquired an individuality through its parliamentary functions. This parliament-assembly of estates created a new solidarity between the members of all the various categories and groups, attributing to them a common responsibility. Moreover, its members also possessed certain rights, besides such obligations as attendance and concession of grants: the right to adjudicate and limit government requests and make their own demands.

At a later stage various limitations and obstacles to the general utility of parliamentary assemblies emerged. But in the early period, from the 12th to the 14th centuries, the novelty was generally welcomed and parliament represented a useful intermediary body between the sovereigns and the most important leaders of the country.

Naturally parliamentary action was subject to various limitations which conditioned its efficacy and even its existence. Above all, parliament was convoked by the sovereign's act of will which, although not arbitrary, remained within his discretion. In consequence, periodic convocations only occurred in so far as they appeared of use to the sovereign. Even if a certain regularity of meetings existed, it was not automatic but remained dependent on the king's will. If he failed to respect the legal or customary interval, his subjects could only protest respectfully; they could not oblige him to issue a writ of summons. The most effective influence on the king's decision was his evaluation of the reciprocal concessions or *octrois* between king and parliament, between government and estates. But the choice was his.

A further limitation was that at a certain point this representative organ of the subjects found itself bound and constrained by a regime of almost unlimited dependence of subjects on their monarchs. Nevertheless, even after the medieval ideology of consent had been abandoned, parliaments continued to exist. They undoubtedly appeared as instruments of conservation, and unquestionably they frequently lost the sense of their representative functions. But they did not only act in defence of particularist interests, they also attempted to resist the increasing tendency of governments to escape from any check or control of their subjects.

Notes

1. See Document D., p. 143.—Ed.
2. Marongiu cites Howard Lord, "The Parliaments of the Middle Ages and the Early Modern Period," *Catholic Historical Review*, XVI (1930), 125-144.

Chapter 15 COUNSEL AND CONSENT IN CAPETIAN ASSEMBLIES OF THE 12TH AND 13TH CENTURIES

One of the few scholars to have dealt with royal and feudal consultation as a subject in its own right rather than as parliamentary "pre-history" is G. I. LANGMUIR (b. 1924). Canadian by birth, he received his graduate training at Harvard and has taught at Stanford University since 1955. The reader should consider carefully how Professor Langmuir's argument below is related to those in the other selections gathered in this section.

The historians who have recently been concerned with the nature and development of French royal assemblies have directed their attention primarily to the period after 1300. The eleventh and twelfth centuries have been neglected, and the thirteenth century has been looked at from the perspective of the fourteenth century rather than the twelfth. The picture of eleventh and twelfth century assemblies that Luchaire and Langlois elaborated about the turn of the century, which was taken over almost unaltered by the later legal historians, Esmein, Chénon, Declareuil, and Olivier-Martin, remains the accepted description today. Yet that picture needs, I believe, substantial revision and supplementation. Constructed by historians mainly interested in the development of institutions and royal power, it

From Gavin Langmuir, "Counsel and Capetian Assemblies," *Xe Congrès international des Sciences historiques: Études présentées à la Commission Internationale pour l'Histoire des Assemblées d'États*, XVIII (Louvain, 1958), 21-34 (abridged; footnotes omitted). Reprinted by permission of the author.

exaggerates the extent to which assemblies were a defined institution, attributes the existence of assemblies too exclusively to the will of the monarchy, and neglects one of the most obvious yet least examined characteristics of royal assemblies, that they were, for contemporaries, primarily occasions on which counsel was given and taken.

The two main features of the accepted description deserve attention. In the first place, all royal assemblies are described as activities of an institution, the *curia regis*; and the duty of counsel, which explains the attendance of the magnates, is defined institutionally as service of court, whether to advise or to judge. Secondly, the existence of assemblies is attributed to royal initiative and political necessity: the early Capetians, it is said, convoked assemblies, not because of a legal or moral obligation, but because assemblies were necessary to gain vassalic cooperation when the monarchy was too weak to act independently.

The first point, that all early assemblies were courts, or aspects of the *curia regis*, is clearly stated by Luchaire.[1] He noted that contemporaries in fact used a variety of terms for assemblies: *curia, concilium, conventus, colloquium, synodus,* and *placitum.* But despite that evidence of contemporary diversity, he felt able to state that, "Basically it was the same court, with differences in the number and quality of those present, which played in turn the role of council, tribunal, council of war, and electoral, administrative, or political assembly". He concluded his discussion of early assemblies with the ringing assertion that, "The *curia generalis* of Louis VII was thus going to end, by a natural evolution, in those solemn assizes of the time of John the Good and Charles VI, in which one sees the bourgeoisie struggle so valiantly to assure for our country the system of free representation and the constitutional guarantees without which there can be neither lasting greatness nor prosperity for a nation". In these nationalistic and somewhat Darwinian phrases, the view is fully developed that the origin of political assemblies is to be sought primarily in the development of a royal institution, the *curia regis*.

The same identification of assemblies with the court, using the contemporary term *curia regis*, was made by Langlois: "For another century after Louis the Fat, the Capetian Court . . . as tribunal, and the Court, as assembly of pomp or political assembly, kept its general name of *Curia Regis* . . .". Petit-Dutaillis and William Newman also described assemblies as meetings of the court. The same view has been repeated recently by Fawtier: "Until the death of St. Louis the sovereign governs alone with the help of a few familiars. In case of need he has recourse to the *Curia*, to the great vassals; but this recourse is in no way obligatory, and is, moreover, not frequent".

The propriety of this use of the term *curia regis* for assemblies is a little dubious, since the variety of contemporary terminology suggests that contemporaries did not think of assemblies in any clear and consistent way. Yet, provided that Luchaire, Fliche, Newman, and Petit-Dutaillis were right in maintaining that contemporaries did not distinguish between the various terms used for assemblies, then the only danger in this somewhat arbitrary use of the term *curia regis* is that it gives a misleading sense of definition to something remarkably vague and implies that contemporaries were clearly conscious of all assemblies as part of a recognizable, defined institution. If, however, contemporaries did not use all these terms interchangeably, but distinguished certain kinds of assemblies, then the description of all assemblies as activities of the *curia regis* would be not simply misleading but unacceptable. . . .

In the last half of the twelfth century and the first half of the thirteenth, a period for which the evidence is far clearer, the term *curia, cour,* or *cort* was apparently used in charters, letters, and Latin and vernacular chronicles only in connection with legal and festive activities or to indicate the location of the king and his household. So far as I have been able to discover, *curia* was never used in connection with non-judicial deliberations.

The language that was used to describe non-judicial deliberations indicates that contemporaries did not think of such consultations as formal meetings of any defined group or body, but rather as irregular, *ad hoc*, occasions on which the king took counsel on various matters. In particular, there is nothing to indicate that contemporaries considered the duty of counsel to be service of court or thought of non-judicial consultations as activities or expanded sessions of the *curia regis*. It therefore seems remarkably difficult to maintain that the political assemblies of the thirteenth and fourteenth centuries developed out of the *curia regis* of the later twelfth century. The origin of those assemblies must be sought elsewhere.

The second explanation of early assemblies, that they were primarily a royal expedient, and that their origin is to be sought in the practical political needs of a weak monarchy is also unsatisfactory because one-sided. It neglects the political interests of the magnates and overlooks the whole mental atmosphere of the period. Before we can use a weak monarchy's need for vassalic cooperation to explain the fact that the magnates cooperated, we must understand the beliefs that predisposed the magnates to accept the duty of counsel as a valid obligation and to cooperate in this particular fashion. There is no doubt that consultations were a valuable political device for the monarchy; what is too often forgotten is that they were also the fulfillment of an ancient royal obligation which the magnates were interested in preserving. On this point, the historians concerned with the way medieval men thought are in almost direct opposition to the institutional and legal historians of French assemblies. For Bloch, like Carlyle and Kern, has stressed that, "According to the code of good government then universally acknowledged, no chief, whoever he might be, could decide anything important without having taken counsel".

That obligation to give and take counsel was an old obligation with deep roots. The obligation to give counsel existed before the creation of feudal law and later became incorporated into feudalism as one of the two positive duties of the vassal. The obligation to take counsel is already explicitly enunciated in the statements of

Lothaire of France, Abbo of Fleuri, and Hugh Capet . . . that a king could not and should not rule without the counsel of his magnates. It is still very much alive two centuries later, as can be seen in Rigord's description of Philip Augustus as accustomed always to use the counsel and wisdom of the archbishops, bishops, and greater princes of the kingdom in his frequent affairs requiring deliberation—and we might note that Rigord does not speak of the advice of the *curia*. The enduring importance of the obligation to give and take counsel is undeniable, but the reason for its importance is less evident.

Why does counsel confront us in canon law, in charter after charter, and on page after page of the chronicles in connection with a multitude of decisions in all areas of life from the convent to the battlefield? Although there is only too abundant evidence of the use of counsel, *consilium* has never received the attention that has been paid to its companion term *auxilium*.[2] The historians of political theory have discussed it, but, because of their concern with the medieval conception of law and law-making, they limited their examination of counsel to that context and, by a thorough confusion of counsel and consent, described counsel as a peculiar kind of community ratification or assent. A broader and more thorough examination of counsel seems necessary to improve our understanding of the contemporary conception of decision-making and our understanding of assemblies and their development. The closely allied problem of the nature of consent also needs further examination, but it must be neglected here.

The distinction between counsel and consent is, however, important for an understanding of contemporary attitudes towards counsel. For despite occasional confusions in specific contexts, *consilium* and *consensus* or *assensus* were normally differentiated both in church and lay thought and practice in this period.[3] A superior might seek counsel to ensure the wisdom of any kind of decision, but he had to seek consent only when the execution of a decision would infringe the rights of others in order to make the decision legally applicable to them. When the king took counsel on a decision that did not affect the rights of others but fell clearly within his acknowledged rights, it was the king who, through consultation, decided what he should do; and it was his exercise of his rights in commanding the necessary actions which gave his decision legal force. No consent was necessary. Any attempt to understand royal consultations should, therefore, differentiate between the very many occasions on which the king sought counsel and the remarkably rare occasions on which he also sought consent. For governing, in all its aspects, was far more than the definition or application of law; many decisions were severely practical and only related to existing rights most indirectly. For such decisions the king did not need consent, but on many of them he took counsel.

The core of the feudal conception of counsel, as it had developed by the end of the twelfth century, is perhaps best captured in the praise of William Marshal by Flemish magnates: "Blessed be the counsel of a preudome."[4] The counsel sought in deliberations was apparently expected to be, ideally, the kind of disinterested advice that a man imbued with the chivalric virtues of bravery, loyalty, experience, wisdom, and love of God would give. . . .

As Bloch has said, to understand the attitude of the medieval vassal towards his lord, it is necessary to know also his attitude towards God.

The church chroniclers, less prone to waste parchment on platitudes of baronial morality, nonetheless reveal their conception of counsel by their adjectives. Good counsel was primarily a question of wisdom in their eyes, but bad counsel stemmed from immorality rather than ignorance. Clearly the two main and inextricably intertwined attributes of good counsel were wisdom and consonance with chivalric and religious standards. A man who gave good counsel did not argue self-interestedly, nor was he a flatterer; he declared what he believed wisdom and morality commanded to be done in a particular situation for the honour and well-being of the leader and the group. Wendover sums up this point neatly describing John's familiars who, "desirous of pleasing the king in everything, gave counsel not according to reason but according to will."

Yet group consultation was not thought of as simply a way of making much good counsel available; it was also, apparently, the accepted method for discovering which was the best of the counsels given, and was, consequently, in some sense, a guarantee that the action taken after consultation was the best discoverable action. For not only was it believed that amongst many knowledgeable and concerned persons there would more probably be some whose wisdom, experience, and morality—aided by divine inspiration—would enable them to discover the proper conduct, but it also seems to have been believed that, once the best counsel had been enunciated by one person, all men of good will would then recognize it as such, even though they themselves had been unable to discover it. Nothing is more striking than the frequency with which the chroniclers describe a leader as acting according to the advice—apparently unanimous—of a group. Even on the rare occasions when the chroniclers record a heated discussion, they usually describe the outcome as if the result had been the unanimous recognition of the value of one counsel. That the counsel finally accepted was usually that of a powerful member of the group, and that its acceptance was largely a result of his influence, would not have seemed to contemporaries a blatant contradiction with their values because of their respect for age, authority, and experience.

The likelihood of unanimity was further increased by the tendency to interpret continuing dissent as a sign of evil character or invincible ignorance. Certainly the explanation of dissent by casting aspersions on the morality of the opposition is not uniquely medieval, but it was particularly inevitable in a period which believed firmly in a divinely ordered hierarchic universe, which condemned the play of self-interest and excluded the contest of politics as we know it from its accepted principles. In such a period, in which specialization was a late arrival, even in the field of law, dissent was schism and a sign of enmity. "Know," said Henry II, "that

I do not wish nor do I have the power to withdraw from the counsel of my kingdom, lest I be seen to nourish schism and discord in the kingdom." . . .

With this conception of consultation as the best means for discovering the best course of action, the magnates naturally expected the king to take counsel with them before any important or unusual action. For, although in giving counsel they did not give consent or additional legal force, in the narrow sense, to royal commands, they did help to ensure that the king would exercise his rights wisely and well. That the king exercise his rights wisely and well was indeed a central principle of lawful government, but one of that intangible medieval variety which could be tested in no court and had no sanction save the judgment of God in heaven and, on earth, rebellion or simple non-cooperation. Yet because of that principle, the king was under a moral obligation, which long custom and political necessity reinforced, to reach important decisions by consulting his natural counsellors, the magnates lay and ecclesiastical.

In fact the Capetians consulted their magnates on most major decisions and were rarely opposed in these consultations. That lack of opposition, it may be suggested, is evidence not so much of the political incompetence of the magnates as of the extent to which common beliefs were favourable to an increase of royal power. For the increase of royal power to the end of St. Louis' reign was achieved not by any radical change in the form of existing rights or in the prevailing conception of law or monarchy, but by a skillful utilization of prevailing beliefs concerning the right government of the kingdom, by making those royal rights which were already acknowledged in theory a reality in practice.

In this achievement, royal-baronial consultations proved extremely useful to the monarchy because medieval attitudes towards decision-making emphasized the good of the whole at the expense of the good of the parts, because the atmosphere of consultation influenced the magnates to state, agree unanimously with, and promise support for just those generally accepted principles concerning the good of the whole kingdom and its chief representative and guardian that the monarchy wished to enforce. Yet once the monarchy had gained outstanding power and stature by these traditional means, the ancient royal obligation to consult became highly susceptible to modification precisely because consultation had never been legally or institutionally defined but had remained an irregular expression of a set of attitudes which were certain to change with a changing society. During the thirteenth century, the development of professional jurists and bureaucrats and the impact of effective royal power, internal peace, and the personality of St. Louis, made the monarchy seem ever more clearly the chief representative of the whole community and the principal source of wisdom and morality. The importance attached to baronial counsel declined correspondingly. Yet the fourteenth century was to show that, although the old belief in the wisdom and morality of the community was declining, it was by no means dead.

Notes

1. Langmuir cites Achille Luchaire, *Histoire des institutions monarchiques*, 2d ed. (Paris, 1891), I, 265.—Ed.
2. See below, Document B, p. 142.—Ed.
3. Langmuir here quotes the decretist Huguccio of Pisa; his citation is given below, p. 143, Document E.2, together with the text of Gratian's *Decretum* on which Huguccio's comment is based.—Ed.
4. "Good man."—Ed.

Chapter 16 THE MILITARY SETTING FOR EARLY PARLIAMENTARY EXPERIENCE

To THOMAS N. BISSON, author of *Assemblies and Representation in Languedoc in the Thirteenth Century* (Princeton, 1964) and a professor of medieval history in the University of California (Berkeley), it seemed that the discussion of the origins of medieval parliamentarism had taken too little account of the circumstances of societies organized primarily for war. In reading the article excerpted below, the student should consider critically how its author understands the concept of "origins" as well as his specific arguments for military influence.

Among the circumstances that attended the formation of parliamentary institutions in the Middle Ages, one seldom hears of militarism or military organization. The prevailing understanding comprises such factors as the persistence of feudal traditions of counsel and law, the emergence of an urban class, the revival of Roman legal principles of public responsibility and representation, and the ever more urgent financial needs of expanding governments. It is not my purpose to reject this pattern of explanation. On the contrary, I should like for the present to assume that it is generally satisfactory. But it seems to me that militarism has been unduly neglected in accounting for the rise of consultative government and that it should be investigated as a fundamental condition to which the well-known factors or "causes" may be related. Fortunately there have been some prospectors in this

From T. N. Bisson, "The Military Origins of Medieval Representation," *American Historical Review*, LXXI (1966), 1199-1218 (abridged; footnotes omitted).

domain; the problem, while neglected, has not passed unnoticed. It will appear that my discussion owes much to suggestions and contributions made by William Stubbs, J. H. Round, J. E. A. Jolliffe, Michael Powicke, and other authorities.

The underestimation of military aspects of parliamentary origins may perhaps be attributed to the tendency to view developments of the High Middle Ages anachronistically. In recent times representative institutions have come to be regarded as incompatible with militarist rule. Ordinary affairs of state are usually distinguished sharply from what we like to think of as the extraordinary affairs of war. Yet it is hardly open to doubt that European representation arose in a society of a different sort: a society that, notwithstanding considerable advances in social objectives and political-administrative techniques, remained organized primarily for war. Even in England, with its exceptionally progressive institutional life, those who ruled were still in the thirteenth century mainly those who fought. Those who *were* ruled, moreover, were still thought of in fundamentally military terms. Landholding, the obligations of society, and privileges long continued to be defined militarily—and no one questions the significance of tenure and status in parliamentary beginnings. The "people" or "nation," considered in relation to the ruler as well as to other peoples, was in the first instance an army, or at any rate the pool from which an army could be mustered. . . .

That the earliest secular assemblies of the Middle Ages were armies is too well known to require much elaboration. Christian Pfister speaks of the Frankish Mayfield as an "assembly" that was "at once an army, a council and a legal tribunal." The chronicles swarm with allusions to army-assemblies, the doings of which offered the best available key to understanding public affairs. Furthermore, without apparently straining their terminology, chroniclers invariably speak of armies as being "assembled," using such words as *convocare, congregare, aggregare, adunare,* and *convenire*. What is perhaps less well known is that armies continued to have a political identity, and assemblies to approximate armies in composition, throughout the Middle Ages. Armies gave counsel on political as well as military affairs, elected monarchs, approved legislation, and (as Fulcher of Chartres says of the army of the First Crusade) were "ruled" by their leaders. . . . The famed peasant democracy of Switzerland was based on common military duties, and in some of the cantons it has remained obligatory to bear weapons to the *Landsgemeinde*[1] down to our own days.

In most parts of Europe, however, the "nation in arms" was always impractical, so that from earliest times armies assumed the character of representations of the people. Military aristocracies, deriving privileges from prowess, were composed of "natural representatives." More significant, because rationally contrived, was the Carolingian device for "selective service" in the host, based on manses. The military representation of hides in Anglo-Saxon England was quite comparable. . . . European armies continued to be composed of token or reduced contingents of nobles against feudal quotas and of urban and rural deputations.

Yet it would be a mistake to argue that armies as such were, or became, "representative institutions" in the proper sense of the term. Despite the continuously ambiguous nature of their convocations, the men of the post-Carolingian epochs knew how to distinguish between military and nonmilitary assemblies, and even better between aid and counsel. What matters, then, is not so much the likeness between armies and assemblies (though that likeness has a further significance to which it will be necessary to return) as the military aspects and interests of convocations that were certainly assemblies in the usual sense.

The assemblies convoked for military purposes were very numerous in the feudal ages from the tenth to the thirteenth century. They constitute, indeed, a large proportion of the royal consultative meetings mentioned by French and English chroniclers. Ferdinand Lot and Robert Fawtier have suggested that the only normal occasion for massive convocations of vassals by the early Capetian monarchs was when military campaigns were to be decided upon or undertaken. The famous defensive muster of Louis VI against the threatened German invasion of 1124 is a case in point. The abbot Suger speaks of a preliminary convocation of nobles in which the "cause" was explained. Then came the rendezvous at Reims, where further discussions, about tactics, took place. Defense and tactics were likewise basic issues in the consultative assemblies of the Norman and Angevin kings of England. Foreign expeditions were also projected in assemblies, in England soon after the Conquest, in France not until the time of Philip Augustus. . . .

There is no need to multiply examples of military assemblies. They occurred everywhere during and after the eleventh century, and like almost all consultations of their time they were quite devoid of institutional characteristics. They were occasions rather than the meetings of definite or recognized bodies, occasions for being briefed, for advising, for approving. Of these functions, counsel was the most important, and there is more to be learned that was of lasting significance in the development of parliamentary institutions by studying the prevailing idea of counsel in these assemblies than by attempting to generalize about summonses, composition, and procedure.

Consilium, deeply rooted in theology, psychology, and law,[2] had come to be understood almost instinctively as the way to wisdom for fallible men. I need not dwell here on the diversities of this complicated term: its meaning as a moral imperative, or as a legal obligation or right, or its meaningful early confusion with the word *concilium*. What is important to notice is that, in the lay practice of the Middle Ages, counsel is mentioned with exceptional frequency in military situations. This was only natural in a warlike society, to be sure, and it satisfactorily explains why counsel very early took its place with aid (*auxilium*)—meaning, primarily, military aid—as one of the two basic services required by feudal lords from their vassals.

It should be stressed that *consilium* and *auxilium* were quite distinct things.

Historians have done good work in demonstrating the different institutional developments that originated in these obligations. But it has not, to my knowledge, been sufficiently remarked that counsel and aid, even though distinct, were nevertheless closely related to each other. The two terms were habitually linked in common usage. An archbishop of Reims, in doing fealty to the first Capetian kings late in the tenth century, promised "to give them counsel and aid according to my knowledge and ability in all affairs, and not knowingly to help their enemies, either with counsel or with aid." A generation later Bishop Fulbert of Chartres expressed the vassal's positive duties in similar terms, but even more succinctly: that "he faithfully perform counsel and aid for his lord";[3] and the success of Fulbert's classic analysis of the feudal relation probably helped to make "counsel and aid" the idiomatic commonplace it had become by the twelfth century. Apart from their feudal specificity, the associated ideas readily lent themselves to general metaphorical applications. The popularity of the concept they expressed is the more easily understood when we recall the prevailing medieval disposition to glorify personal wisdom and prowess in combination.

Counsel and aid, then, were related. Let us now remark that these related but distinct concepts tended with time to be confused with each other. For this result *auxilium* was chiefly responsible. Semantically the broader term, it was easily taken to mean service (*servitium*) of any kind, including counsel; whereas *consilium*, even though it implied judicial as well as advisory service, could hardly be construed to mean aid in any wider sense.

The assimilation of *consilium* by *auxilium*, so to speak, while widely apparent in charters, in those, for example, of Burgundy and Navarre, can best be seen in the investigations of feudal rights made by kings and lords in the twelfth and thirteenth centuries. I suspect that these investigations have more interest for early parliamentary institutions than historians have realized. The fact is that lists of feudal recognitions usually specify military obligations but not conciliar ones. The *Cartae Baronum*[4] of 1166 were concerned with knight service in England; six years later Henry II obtained analogous information on knights' fees in Normandy. In France the royal inquiries begun under Philip Augustus, though rather diverse in purposes, are especially rich in detail about military duties, some being exclusively military, but they have little to say about conciliar or judicial obligations. The same imbalance manifests itself in southern France and Aragon in the thirteenth century. For instance, in 1259, when 159 nobles of Agenais made recognitions of their fiefs and obligations, only one of them volunteered that he owed "court" as well as homage and knight service to the king.

What is the meaning of the fact thus illustrated? Surely it cannot be simply that feudal counsel was declining in value after about 1150. The same thing, after all, might be said of knight service with almost equal truth. The reasons for this continued emphasis on military obligations, it may be suggested, are somewhat as follows: that military necessities remained paramount in this period; that the obligations denoted by *auxilium* were broad in nature, and easily convertible (into payments of money, for example; this is, indeed, the usual meaning of *auxilium* in the recognition rolls); and that as a matter of practical experience lords who could convoke their men armed for battle could fairly well count on being able to convoke them for other purposes, too. Anyway, what *were* the other reasons for gathering knights in assembly? Those summoned to fight would necessarily convene at the outset, listen to explanations, and give counsel. For nonmilitary policy and ordinary administration the greater lords had little use for vassals en masse; there can be no mistaking the trend toward specialized counsel at the expense of feudal. It is true that there was still need of vassals for judging, the nobles being especially tenacious of their presumed characteristic judiciousness. The theoretical obligation of attendance apparently had its longest life in this sense. Significantly, when this obligation *is* mentioned in feudal investigations, it is usually "court" (*curia*) or "plea" (*placitum*), not *consilium*, that is specified.

Auxilium, therefore, came to mean, or imply, *consilium* in addition to military service; but there is probably another reason why princely officials in the later Middle Ages tended to ignore "counsel" *eo nomine* when recording their dues. It is precisely in the period when such records began to be kept that *consilium* began to be recognized as a right as well as an obligation by the people summoned to give it. This, of course, was a landmark in medieval constitutionalism. When subjects became as interested as rulers in counsel, there was less reason for rulers to make a point of it. Thenceforth it is the custom books, charters, and privileges that can be expected to furnish the best evidence on the principles of consultation. And when we come to consider the military interests of later medieval assemblies, we must be prepared to think of the tradition of counsel both as right and as obligation.

Now I should like to suggest that the notion of counsel that was perpetuated in the councils, parliaments, and representative assemblies after 1215 continued to some appreciable extent to be that of a "military counsel" such as just described. The "peace of the thirteenth century" was often threatened and sometimes broken, and among the more notable convocations to discuss military projects may be mentioned the great courts of Jaime I before the Aragonese conquests of Mallorca and Valencia in 1228 and 1236, and the great council of 1242 in which Henry III of England requested "counsel and aid" for his Gascon campaign. Moreover, the traditional militancy of counsel is sometimes discernible in contemporary references to assemblies whose functions were not obviously military. Of Philip the Fair's celebrated national assembly in 1302 a compiler wrote that "Philip convoked all the nobles and communities of his kingdom to Paris, seeking [their] counsel and aid against all men and . . . especially [their petition was] against the pope." Now while a statement of this sort carries no authority for the official character of the assembly in question, it is of interest as a witness to popular attitudes. And in fact the phrase about counsel and aid was not yet even officially obsolete since it appears in the summonses for the royal assembly of Tours in 1308 (accompanied by the King's declaration that his opposition to the Templars was in the great Capetian tradition of militant defense of the faith). Nor was the chronicler's terminology inappropriate. The assembly of 1302, whatever else it may have been, was palpably a council of war. The Pope was represented as an enemy of the faith and of France, and it was reported that the assembled nobles and town deputies responded to the charges with a pledge to expose their property and lives in defense of the King's rights. However novel in composition and however new the arguments urged in it, the assembly of 1302 was old-fashioned in its belligerency, militant if not military in function.

We are now in a position to appreciate the bearing of military concerns on the development of representation (in the strict sense) and consent. It will be recognized that the "aid" desired in 1242, as on so many other occasions in the later Middle Ages, was primarily financial aid—*auxilium* in its pecuniary meaning. The relevance of this to the present argument is, of course, that the financial aids and scutages, which in England ought to be levied with the "common counsel of the realm,"[5] continued to be taxes for chiefly military purposes. This is not the place to retell the familiar story of how elements more representative than the magnates who originally spoke for the English realm came to be consulted about taxation, nor to discuss the comparable progress on the Continent. While in a sense the military approach brings us into the consensus of modern scholarship that financial powers were among the decisive factors in the development of representation, it is clear that taxation had ordinarily but a contingent relation to military functions. The essential point lies deeper than this. When C. H. McIlwain reminds us that what kings and princes usually wanted from the townsmen they summoned was aid (and not counsel),[6] we should bear in mind that the fundamental aid of most medieval towns—the obligatory *auxilium* of urban custom as of knightly—was active military service. For in the first place the aid requested in such assemblies was sometimes service itself rather than money. Secondly, a whole class of impositions, notably the scutages and fines, were undisguised commutations of service, and hence not, strictly speaking taxes at all. . . . Thirdly, even when, as was more commonly the case, the aid in prospect was a pecuniary levy, the military urgency or liability could be so forcibly stressed as to render its payment virtually a purchase of exemption from service. This is illustrated by the carefully worded writs of 1254 ordering the summons of representative knights in England to grant aid for the threatened war with Castille. A lengthy preamble details the dangerous service to which magnates and twenty-pound tenants in chief were committed, thus making it appear to the other men of the counties that a good payment was but a fair and desirable contribution on their part. On the other hand, active military service provided an important basis of exemption from the new lay subsidies of Edward I in the years when they came under parliamentary control. In short, though the *auxilium* or *servitium* tendered by representative elements undoubtedly broadened in meaning in early consultative experience, its basis and associations were strongly military in origin.

The concept of consent likewise assumes significance in the thirteenth century. Not that consent as distinct from counsel was entirely new in the military councils of this period. It is probable that earlier practice had conformed in a general way to the principle that, whereas defensive wars and field strategy required no more than a prudent consultation or notification of the vassal-warriors, the undertaking of foreign expeditions and offensive wars necessitated obtaining their consent. Orderic Vital, in a remarkable passage that distinguishes clearly between counsel, council, and consent, vividly describes the assembly at Winchester in 1089 in which the magnates "gave their assent" to William Rufus' proposal to send an army to Normandy. Other instances could be cited, especially in connection with taxation and extraordinary service. It seems unlikely, nevertheless, that consent was yet an important function in military councils before the great development of taxation in the thirteenth century. Not even in 1215, in that section of their petition which became Chapter XII of Magna Carta, were the barons demonstrably interested in the juridical character of the "common counsel" they sought for the levy of aids and scutages. But the trouble with counsel, as the next generation came ruefully to realize, was that it could be ignored even when it had to be asked. Moreover, kings proved to be less prudent about requesting money for projected wars than about committing themselves to lead armies to battle. The result was that rulers like Henry III, Edward I, and Philip IV found themselves increasingly obliged to obtain consent as well as counsel in their assemblies and negotiations. But they also found that consent was adaptable to requirements of the new age of international war, capable of growing with the realm itself to the recognition of common responsibility for national necessity.

These traditions of military counsel, representation, and consent were confirmed in the parliamentary institutions of the fourteenth century. By the reign of Edward III military matters were understood to be foremost among the *negotia regni*[7] in which the English parliament had obtained an authoritative voice. The writs of military summons now regularly mention the approval of Parliament to wars and campaigns proposed by the king. A rather similar development occurred in Spain. In France, where the constitutional situation differed in important respects, the general Estates of Languedoïl likewise had acquired by the 1350's, or rather were enjoying for the moment, extensive powers in military policy and finance. . . .

The foregoing points can be further illustrated from the history of the crusades and of nonfeudal and local experience. . . .

The Council of Clermont in 1095—the first of a long series of major political convocations for "taking the cross"—was also an assembly of the Peace and Truce of God. It would be difficult to exaggerate the importance of the peace movements for the rise of representation in the turbulent regions between the Ebro River and the Loire. The Catalan Cortes emerged directly from the peace councils of the twelfth century, and the traditional statutes of *pax et treuga* were still being promulgated in the maturing general courts of the later thirteenth century. In the uplands of Languedoc several regions became spheres of associative interest centering upon the maintenance of peace through discussion, taxation, and punitive military campaigns. The bishop of Mende summoned representative contingents of parishioners when the castle-based gangsters of Gévaudan caused trouble, and it seems reasonably clear that the peace armies there sometimes doubled as assemblies. The custom of Quercy called for separate negotiations whenever the peace was broken, in diocesan assemblies that included representative townsmen. And if peace institutions did not develop vigorously in the valley of the lower Garonne, it was because their function was discharged by a secular assembly called the "general court" of Agenais, which originated in the twelfth century. Composed of nobles and the deputies of towns and villages, this curious little meeting—one of the earliest representative institutions of the Middle Ages—had as its primary business the judgment of disputes that threatened the peace of the countryside. When necessary the assembly, or its presiding official, would order out the "general army" of Agenais, a force that evidently approximated the court in composition.[8] These diverse forms of military consultation constituted significant precedents for the French provincial Estates. . . .

Enough has now been said of the bellicose functions of assemblies, perhaps more than enough. It will be necessary, indeed, to qualify some of the points made thus far in order to assess their significance fully. Before doing this, however, it may be well simply to acknowledge the occurrence, ever more frequent, of assemblies that functioned in peaceful, nonmilitary ways. For it remains to notice that in one remarkable respect these assemblies as well as military ones—in fact, many assemblies, regardless of purpose—were influenced from the military quarter. To put it briefly, assemblies presented the men who convoked them with the same administrative problem as armies; how to summon them and whom to summon. . . . (In the section which follows, it is argued that the summons to assemblies was often patterned on the summons to armies, not only in regard to the form of the writs but also in the determination, recorded in administrative lists, of whom to summon.)

Most of the military influences . . . assumed renewed importance in the fourteenth century—an epoch of renewed conflict. In function as in form the assemblies of the later Middle Ages were significantly oriented to military requirements. But this was no simple reversion to the rough parliamentarism of the early feudal age. Assemblies had in the meantime acquired notable functions of nonmilitary kinds, particularly during the relatively peaceful decades of the thirteenth century, and these functions were not lost thereafter. It may be argued that the most successful assemblies from a constitutional point of view, such as the Cortes and the English Parliament, were precisely those which had proved capable of developing their powers in peace as well as in war. Yet even the nonbelligerent attributes, we should remember, were fostered by the exigencies of war. Taxation has already been mentioned in this connection, and political and judicial activities are also in point. The propagandistic uses of early assemblies, to which Taylor and J. R. Strayer have directed our attention, are most evident in time of war; while, according to the suggestion of Gaines Post, Parliaments of Edward I were, in a legal sense, sitting in judgment on the King's "case" for military support. Plainly it will not do to think of war in a narrowly military sense. The political aspects of war attained increasing prominence in the assemblies of the twelfth and thirteenth centuries as rulers, helped by the progressive ordering of their peoples within definite and defensible boundaries, gained better control of the wars they fought. Some of the assemblies mentioned in preceding pages were "military" only, or chiefly, in this political sense. As the engrossing immediacy of warfare begins to give way before governmental progress, moreover, a certain archaism or formalism becomes perceptible in some of the specifically military aspects of late medieval consultation. The use of military lists in constituting parliaments possibly indicates administrative conservatism as much as political necessity. And the militant feudal terms that persist in writs and descriptions of assemblies evoke a strain of traditional thought about consultation that was beginning to lose its relevance in the new royal politics of the fourteenth century. But it was only much later that armies and their interests drastically broke with assemblies. The modern inheritance of legislative control over standing armies and war appropriations is a much-reduced remnant of the military accumulation in medieval representative institutions.

A military and political reality, medieval warfare was also, in the final analysis, a social phenomenon. Its institutions resembled those of consultation in being incidents of a massive organizing of society. How to classify, how to record, how to mobilize or manage: these had come to be the meaningful questions, and they had in common a relevance for military and conciliar problems. The sociolegal changes that determined these administrative questions, such as the "territorializing" (that is, standardizing) of obligations, the consolidation of nobility, and the emergence of an urban class, had a still more evident mutual significance. But this organizing and defining served a kind of social leverage that was ordained primarily to the needs of coercive power. Well might the management of assemblies rest content with its military schooling; so too, in different ways, the appearance of military orders of clergy and the anxious persistence in fortifying cities real and imagined seem symptomatic. The pervasive experience of war—condition as well as cause—forms a social perspective in which the rise of medieval representation can be better understood.

Notes

1. "Regional assembly."—Ed.
2. See below, Document A, p. 141.—Ed.
3. See below, Document B, p. 142.—Ed.
4. "Charters of the Barons."—Ed.
5. Document F, p. 144; though these clauses were omitted from reissues of the Charter, they continued to be observed in practice.—Ed.
6. See above, p. 56.
7. "Business of the realm."—Ed.
8. See Document C, p. 143.—Ed.

Chapter 17 THE ECCLESIASTICAL SETTING FOR MEDIEVAL CONSTITUTIONALISM

Among the more comprehensive recent
explanations of medieval parliamentarism is
that of BRIAN TIERNEY (b. 1922),
professor of medieval history at Cornell
University and a specialist in ecclesiastical
thought and canon law. In his presidential
address before the Catholic Historical
Association, from which the present
selection is taken, Professor Tierney speaks
of "constitutionalism" as a phenomenon
broadly and uniquely paramount in
European governments from about
A.D. 1200 to 1400 and stresses the ecclesiastical contribution to that phenomenon.

... During the past twenty years an extensive literature has grown up concerning
the ecclesiology and political theories of the Decretists and Decretalists. We are
beginning, not only to understand the general outlines of their thought, but to
appreciate the individual characteristics of many particular teachers, of men like
Huguccio, Alanus, Laurentius, Hostiensis, great masters in their own day, whose
names are just beginning to creep into the textbooks on medieval history. My own
intention is not to present yet another technical paper on some detailed point of
canonical scholarship but rather to attempt a broad survey of the significance of all
this recent work for a central problem of Western history—the emergence of the
constitutional state in the Middle Ages. I should be especially happy if I could
succeed in conveying to you that the objective of modern canonistic studies is not

From Brian Tierney, "Medieval Canon Law and Western Constitutionalism," *Catholic Historical
Review*, LII (1966), 1-17 (abridged; footnotes omitted). Reprinted by permission of the author
and of The Catholic University of America Press.

simply to add a few additional esoteric footnotes to the standard works on constitutional history, but rather to find fresh answers for the new problems concerning the nature and origins of constitutionalism that are posed inescapably by the circumstances of our own age.

I am using the word "constitutionalism" to signify simply the most basic, taken-for-granted ideas that are implied by the most familiar platitudes of our political discourse, by phrases like "government under law" or "government by consent." We mean, I take it, a system in which the citizen is guaranteed due process of law and in which law itself is not merely the arbitrary will of a despot but rather reflects the moral outlook of the whole society, at least in its broad principles. And "government by consent," of course, means to us not just that the majority imposes its will on the minority but that machinery exists for eliciting a consensus of opinion, for formulating courses of action that all the citizens are prepared to accept, even though with differing degrees of enthusiasm. The characteristic institutional machinery for eliciting a consensus in modern constitutional states is the elected representative assembly with effective rights of consent to legislation and taxation.

The point which must strike a contemporary historian most forcefully at the outset is the extreme improbability of this kind of system ever emerging anywhere or persisting if by chance it has emerged. During my own lifetime ancient European peoples that might have known better have willingly handed themselves over to the most revolting forms of despotism and new nations that, a few years ago, were everywhere embarking on brave adventures in constitutional government have usually abandoned the system after a brief period of unsuccessful experimentation. . . . The historian cannot fail to discern that the normal story of human government is indeed one of alternation between different forms of tyranny with occasional interludes of anarchy. All this is not to say that our political system must necessarily be dismissed as a mere freakish aberration in the general history of mankind. Perhaps things will be different in the future. Constitutionalism is the distinctive contribution of Western civilization to the art of government, and, in India, the leaders of half a billion people are still striving—not unsuccessfully so far, though the outcome is unpredictable—to adapt our Western institutions to the needs of an Asiatic society. Constitutionalism may after all represent the main axis of development in the growth of human government for the next thousand years. Or it may not. The historical problem of how constitutional structures of government could first grow into existence is a fascinating one for the scholar precisely because the practical issue of whether such structures can survive and expand is poised so delicately in the modern world.

Now nations first began to organize themselves into constitutional states during the Middle Ages. We can indeed trace an interesting and most important chapter in the pre-history of constitutionalism in the life of certain classical city-states; but the problems of government by consent become so much more complex when one moves from the intimate society of a single little city to an area the size of a nation or a whole continent that they become essentially different in kind and necessitate for their solution a different kind of institutional machinery from any that existed in the ancient world. Individual city-states lacked the principle of representation in anything like its modern form. . . .

In a quite different sphere the anthropologists could point out to us dozens of primitive societies that experience limited government in the sense that they have tribal councils and customary laws. Such institutions are in no way peculiar to the Teutonic peoples of northern Europe. One can find them among West Africans or Red Indians, almost anywhere indeed where the appropriate research has been conducted. . . . Primitive societies provide no real analogue for the constitutional state because they lack most of the essential attributes of the state itself—ordered departments of government, written records, the idea of legislation as a deliberate product of reason and will; and when primitive peoples have outgrown their tribal customs to develop a civilization and a state it has normally taken the form of a despotism, most commonly a theocracy. . . .

In Western Europe, from the twelfth century onward, events took a different turn. A great revival of classical Roman law re-introduced into the feudal world of the West with its countless petty jurisdictions the idea of strong central government exercising broad powers of legislation and taxation for the public welfare. Moreover, the example of the Roman *Corpus Iuris*[1] stimulated the monk Gratian to undertake a major systematization of the law of the Church and, about 1140, he completed his Decretum, an immensely influential work that created an ordered synthesis for the first time out of the chaos of conflicting canons, decretals, and patristic texts that had been accumulating in the Church for a thousand years. The next two centuries saw a great growth of governmental activity, first in the ecclesiastical sphere, then in the secular. Kingdoms built up more sophisticated bureaucracies. There was increased taxation, judicial centralization and, by 1300, a great upsurge of legislative activity. But this growth of centralized government coincided precisely with a growth of constitutional theories and practices. Administrative structures were emerging that we can reasonably call states but for the first time they were constitutional states. It was a major turning point in the history of human government. . . .

The immediate point that I am concerned to make is not over-subtle. A modern institution of representative government like the American senate has no meaningful connection whatsoever with the ancient Roman senate. On the other hand its whole nature and mode of functioning is rooted in an antecedent tradition of parliamentary government—and parliament did not come into existence in ancient Greece or ancient Rome but in medieval England. The fact of the matter is that in 1200 there were no national representative assemblies anywhere and there never had been any, while by 1400 the whole Western Church was engaged in trying to replace papal monarchy with conciliar government, and almost every country from

Scandinavia to Spain and from England to Hungary had produced constitutional documents stating that the ruler was under the law and had experimented with representative assemblies seeking to give effect to that principle. This is the phenomenon of medieval constitutionalism. It is, as I have emphasized, a rare, perhaps a unique phenomenon. There is no general work of synthesis that would explain the whole phenomenon satisfactorily. It is surely interesting enough to deserve an explanation.

Medievalists have always been aware of the importance of constitutional history. It has always been a central theme of our discipline. But they have not always approached it from the point of view that I have been suggesting. On the contrary, when the subject first began to be studied scientifically in the nineteenth century, there was a widespread assumption that a constitutional, representative system was a kind of natural norm of human government, which the English had come to exemplify first because of their innate Anglo-Saxon virtue, but toward which all societies could be expected to progress in due course given a little goodwill and a modicum of elementary education. With that preconception the whole task of explaining the origins of constitutionalism became one of merely documenting the stages by which medieval men pursued this normal and natural course of development from Teutonic tribesmen to members of the House of Commons. This in itself presented some problems, and it is widely held nowadays that William Stubbs, the greatest of the early constitutional historians, presented the stages of development wrongly. Around 1900 revisionists like Maitland and McIlwain began to criticize him. The argument proliferated, and it is still going on. We now have a fantastically elaborate bibliography of hundreds of books and articles devoted to this one question and all the fascinating subsidiary issues that arise out of it—whether the English Parliament was already some kind of representative legislature in 1297 or whether we are so radically to modify our whole view of human progress as to suppose that this felicitous state of affairs did not begin to come about until, say, 1327. The material that has been unearthed in the course of the controversy is invaluable. If there is ever to be a satisfactory account of medieval constitutionalism as a whole the interpretation of English parliamentary records will play a major part in it. But this can hardly come about so long as parliamentary studies are conducted in an insular spirit and are dominated to such an extraordinary degree by the discussion of technical problems arising out of an academic dispute of sixty years ago. They need to be set in a broader perspective.

The study of the law of the universal Church can provide such a perspective. If we set out from the terms of reference that impose themselves in the 1960s, from the surely self-evident premise that constitutionalism is not a normal stage in the evolution of societies but extremely abnormal—its emergence improbable, its extension most difficult, its survival always precarious—then we must ask a new kind of question of the age that first produced it. The obvious question is this. What was abnormal about the Middle Ages? What elements of social organization or economic life were common to all the countries of Western Europe between 1200 and 1400 but peculiar to that medieval civilization as a whole compared to the others that we know of? This kind of question leads straight to the topics for which medieval canonists provide the primary source material. For there is nothing very out of the way about the medieval economy—a primitive agrarian basis diversified by a little commerce. Nor is the technology especially striking—more advanced than we used to think but not really remarkable. Nor is the basic social structure, with prestige accorded to a military aristocracy, highly unusual. It is only when we turn to the ecclesiastical aspects of medieval culture that we encounter situations that are indeed extremely abnormal by the standards of most other civilizations.

When students first come to consider the conflicts of popes and kings in the Middle Ages they are sometimes surprised at the pretensions of both sides. They find it remarkable that popes should claim to depose kings or kings to appoint bishops; but there is really nothing unusual in one ruler aspiring to exercise supreme spiritual and temporal power. That again is a normal pattern of human government. Innumerable societies have been ruled by a god-emperor, a divine king or a chieftain of magical potency. The unusual thing in the Middle Ages was not that certain emperors and popes aspired to a theocratic role but that such ambitions were never wholly fulfilled. There remained always two structures of government, ecclesiastical and secular, intricately interlinked but dedicated ultimately to different ends, often in conflict with one another, each constantly limiting the other's power. Evidently the very existence of such a situation would enhance the possibilities for a growth of human freedom by preventing medieval society from congealing into a rigid despotism, and Lord Acton pointed this out long ago. "To that conflict of four hundred years," he wrote, "we owe the rise of civil liberty."

But, although important, this is only part of the story. We have to deal with two societies that were not only frequently in conflict with each other but that were also in a state of constant interaction. Throughout the Middle Ages there was a very frequent interchange of personnel and also of ideas and institutional techniques between the spheres of ecclesiastical and secular government. Kings were anointed like bishops and bishops became feudal lords like kings. Secular laws relating to the ancient Senate were used to define the status of cardinals in the Roman church, and canonical rules regarding the choice of bishops were used to regulate the elections of emperors. The pope assumed the imperial tiara, and the emperor the episcopal mitre. One could multiply such examples endlessly.

To understand the distinctive characteristics of medieval government, therefore, we have to consider two sets of problems—problems of conflict and problems of interaction between Church and State. On the whole the problems of interaction are more complex and more important, and these are the ones that I want particularly to consider. It is quite easy to see in the abstract that a very duality of Church and State in any society would produce a situation of exceptional flexibility. It is very difficult to explain in the concrete how that particular ecclesiastical organization interacted with that particular system of secular government to produce the new forms of constitutional organization whose origins we are trying to explore. Merely to mix ecclesiastical autocracy with feudal anarchy does not sound very promising, and it was widely assumed until recently that all canonical theories of papal authority were indeed starkly autocratic. But a major conclusion arising out of all the recent research is that medieval canon law was not merely, as it was once called, "a marvellous jurisprudence of spiritual despotism." On detailed investigation we find that the great canonistic glosses and *summae* of the age of Innocent III contain, not only the familiar and expected passages exalting papal authority, but also other sections that are filled with constitutional concepts, with sophisticated discussions on representation and consent and on the due limits to lawfully constituted authority, even papal authority.

Before we turn to this structure of ideas we ought to consider a preliminary question that inevitably presents itself. How could medieval canon lawyers, of all people, have been led to pioneer in the development of constitutional principles, of all things? To understand this we must consider one more way in which Western history has pursued an unusual course—I mean in the extraordinary convolutions of its chronological structure. Perhaps no other civilization, through the centuries of its existence, has enjoyed so many and such varied love affairs with its own past as those of the Western world, ranging as they do from the most prolific unions to the merest illicit flirtations. From the twelfth century onward there were all those Renaissances of ancient culture that historians delight in multiplying until, the wheel coming full circle, the Middle Ages themselves became an object of flirtatious advances from the Romantics of the nineteenth century. To the historian, for whom time is the very raw material of his craft, the situation is one of intriguing complexity. For us the essential point is that, in the first great encounter of Western man with his past, the "Renaissance of the twelfth century," a revival of classical Roman law coincided precisely with a new systematic study of all the ancient Christian sources assembled in Gratian's Decretum. Roman law reintroduced the ideas of sovereignty and the state into the Western world but the canonical texts had a distinctive contribution to make too. Early Christianity was not just a belief, but a body of believers, a communion, a community. The earliest references to Christian life are full of community meetings, community sharings, community participation in decisions, community election of officers. Something of this had persisted down to the twelfth century in that the Church was still a structure of elective offices, and the early tradition was reflected very strongly in many of the texts assembled by Gratian.

It would be tempting to assert simply that the first formulation of the basic concepts of Western constitutionalism was stimulated by an encounter between the Roman law idea of a sovereign state and the patristic ideal of a corporate Christian community in the works of the medieval canonists. But this would not be quite the whole truth. After all there was classical law and Christian doctrine in the ancient world and they led on only to Byzantine absolutism. We have to deal with ancient law and early Christian institutions as they were perceived by the eyes of medieval men. . . .

One of the most familiar platitudes of our textbooks is the assertion that Western culture was formed from a fusion of classical and Christian elements. It is true of course like most platitudes. But the textbooks do not always emphasize sufficiently that often the fusion took place in the Middle Ages, and still less that in the fields of law and government the works of the medieval canonists played a crucially important role in the whole process. Yet it could hardly have been otherwise. The canonists were the only group of intellectuals in Western history who were professionally concerned with classical law and with Christian doctrine to an equal degree. They delighted in applying to the papal office all the exalted language which Roman law used in describing the majesty of the emperor. They called the pope a supreme legislator whose very will was law, a supreme judge from whom there could be no appeal, a "lord of the world," "loosed from the laws" . . . They were up against the very nub of the problem of sovereignty. It is easy enough to avoid a despotism if one is content to tolerate an anarchy. The difficult task is to concede to a ruler all the very great powers needed for effective government while guarding against the dangers of arbitrary tyranny.

The canonists' approach to this problem was to seek in the consensus of the whole Christian community, in the indefectible Church guided by the Holy Spirit, norms of faith and order which could define the limits within which the pope's supreme legislative and judicial powers were to be exercised. (The English parliamentary leaders of a later age would set themselves an analogous task in relation to the political community and the limitations of secular kingship.) A juridical basis for the canonists was provided by a text of Pope Gregory the Great, incorporated in the Decretum at Dist. 15 c.2, which declared that the canons of the first four General Councils were always to be preserved inviolate because they were established "by universal consent" or "by a universal consensus". . . . The canonists gave a more precise meaning to Gregory's vague dictum by interpreting it in terms of their own categories of corporation law. They glossed it with phrases like these. "No man can withdraw from the common consent of his community," or "What touches all should be approved by all"—this latter text being used to defend the right of lay representatives to attend General Councils when matters of faith were to be discussed. In the years around 1200 it was commonly maintained that even the pope was bound by the canons of General Councils, representing the whole Church, "in matters pertaining to the faith and the general state of the Church." Such a doctrine could be developed without any attack on the ancient principle of papal primacy because of course the pope himself was normally the presiding head of a General Council. Its canons could be regarded as manifestations of the papal will expressed in its highest, most sovereign form and so as binding on the pope himself considered as an isolated individual. The English canonist who, toward

1200, declared that "the authority of a pope with a council is greater than that of a pope without one" was expressing the same idea that King Henry VIII of England would apply to the secular sphere some three centuries later when he said, "We be informed by our judges that we at no time stand so highly in our estate royal as in time of Parliament wherein we as head and you as members are conjoined and knit together in one body politic."

There remained the possibility of an irreconcilable conflict between the pope and the representatives of the Christian community assembled in a General Council. The canonists of the early thirteenth century were deeply divided over this question but the more radical of them taught that a pope could be corrected and even deposed by a council if his conduct endangered the "state of the church." Fifty years later we find the barons of England claiming the right to oppose their king in defense of the "state of the realm." Long ago historians came to realize that the canonists influenced the history of Western political thought in that their theories of papal sovereignty provided an archetype for later theories of divine right monarchy. We are just beginning to understand the importance of their work for theories of representative government also.

It is a complicated task to reconstruct all the constitutionalist elements in the canonists' thought from their voluminous but scattered glosses, and still more complicated to explain in detail how their ideas influenced the growth of secular government. Basically there were two processes at work. Most obviously the canonists offered reflections on the constitutional law of the Church which could and did influence subsequent speculations on the right ordering of the State. But they also formulated a series of doctrines in the sphere of private law which eventually proved of the utmost importance in the growth of representative government although, at first, they had nothing to do with high matters of state. These private-law doctrines again reflected the collegial structure of the medieval Church. Much of the canonists' day-to-day business dealt with the affairs of ecclesiastical communities. They were therefore led to develop an elaborate jurisprudence concerning the representation of corporate groups, the prerogatives of the head of a juridical society in relation to its members, and the rights of individual members in relation to the whole community before such matters began to be discussed as overt issues of political theory.

Just as in some primitive economies there is a shortage of good currency, so too in the medieval polity there was a shortage of good law, especially of constitutional law. When the need for more sophisticated structures of public law came to be urgently felt men naturally turned to the legal rules that were already available in the province of private law-especially in the well-developed canonical law of corporations-and applied them in the constitutional sphere also. A typical line of development was the assimilation of technical rules of Roman private law into canon law, the subsequent inflation of such rules into general principles of church government by the canonists, and the eventual transfer of those principles to the public law of the growing states by the usual medieval process of osmosis. For instance the already mentioned phrase, *Quod omnes tangit ab omnibus approbetur* (What touches all is to be approved by all), was developed from a mere technicality of the Roman law of co-tutorship into a juristic theory about the right relationship between popes and General Councils in the works of the canonists who were writing around 1200. Then, moving from legal theory to real life, we find it in official documents convoking church councils and, finally, by the end of the thirteenth century, it occurs in writs of summons to secular representative assemblies.

This is not the occasion for a detailed exploration of all the maze of arguments that has grown up around the phrase *Quod ommes tangit* and around other terms that underwent a similar development—*plena potestas, status, necessitas.* Let me rather try to summarize the over-all effect of the quite exceptional interplay between all the diverse influences that were at work in thirteenth-century legal thought. The most striking result of their interaction was to produce a peculiar ambivalence in all the concepts commonly used in medieval political discourse. The ruler's power was conceived of as flowing from both God *and* the people. It was held to be in some ways above the law and in some ways below it. The medieval term *status*, the origin of our "state," was used to extend the authority of rulers by justifying extraordinary or extra-legal actions undertaken by them for the defense of the community, but it also served to define a condition of public welfare that the ruler himself was not permitted to disrupt. Representation could mean either the symbolizing of a community in its head, with absolutist implications, or a delegation of authority from the subjects, with constitutionalist implications. The doctrine of natural law provided both a stimulus to new legislation and a criterion for judging its value. It is not that we find popes and princes, intent on building up centralized power, using one set of concepts, and subjects, intent on limiting that power, using another. The very concepts that all had in common were ambivalent; every building block of sovereignty had a constitutional face; Western political thought was already beginning to revolve around the central problem, or paradox, that has fascinated its greatest exponents ever since, the problem of reconciling the idea of sovereignty with the ideal of limited government, of government "under the law."

Some scholars will think that ideas and ideals have little enough to do with the growth of governmental institutions. One young expert has recently observed that, "It did not matter too much what one or another theorist said. . . ." And, certainly, we could all agree that, when medieval kings summoned representative assemblies, they were not normally inspired to do so by protracted meditations on the subtleties of canonical jurisprudence. Kings needed help or counsel or money. They wanted assent to their policies and political support for them. These obvious facts should indeed receive due emphasis in any institutional history of the Middle Ages, but it is a delusion to suppose that, by merely calling attention to them, we are providing a sufficient explanation for the rise of medieval constitutionalism. The problem of maximizing assent to governmental policies arises for all rulers in all societies. It is not normally solved by the development of representative assemblies. Our argument is not that hard-headed medieval statesmen behaved in such-and-such a way because some theorist in a university had invented a theory saying that they ought to do so. The argument is rather that all men behave in certain ways in part at least because they adhere to certain ways of thinking. No doubt the ideas that are most influential in shaping actions are ones that the agent is hardly conscious of at all—he takes them so much for granted. But the historian has to make himself conscious of those ideas if he is to understand the men of a past age and the institutions that they created. The works of the medieval canonists provide invaluable source material for the constitutional historian precisely because they can help him to become aware of the implicit pre-suppositions about man and society that lay below the surface of medieval political thought and political action. . . .

Notes

1. "Body of law" (Justinian's)—Ed.

Part Six

SOME DOCUMENTARY EVIDENCE

A. *The Benedictine Idea of Counsel**

(Chapter 3) As often as any important business arises in the monastery, let the abbot convoke the entire congregation and let him explain the matter himself. And upon hearing the counsel of the brothers, let him reflect by himself and then do what he judges the more useful. Now we have said that all should be summoned to counsel because the Lord often reveals the better course to the younger person. So let the brothers give counsel with all humble deference and not presume to defend their positions obstinately; instead let the matter depend on the abbot's judgment, so that what he judges to be more salutary may be accepted obediently by all. But

*From *The Rule of Saint Benedict*, ed. Justin McCann (Westminster, Md.: The Newman Press, 1952), chapters 3, 5. Tr. by ed. (abridged).

just as it is fitting for disciples to obey their master, so is it right that he in turn dispose all things prudently and justly. ... The abbot himself, however, should do all things in the fear of God and observance of the Rule, knowing that he shall certainly have to render account for all his judgments to God the most just judge. But when lesser matters are to be dealt with for the monastery's interest, let him refer only to the counsel of the elder monks, as it is written: "Do all things with counsel and you will not repent later."[1]

... (Chapter 5) The first grade of humility is obedience without delay. ...

B. Fulbert of Chartres, *On the Counsel and Aid of Vassals (1020)**

To the glorious duke of the Aquitanians Guillaume, Fulbert [sends] the voice of prayer.

Asked to write something about the form of fealty (*fidelitas*), I have briefly noted for you, on the authority of books, the following things. He who swears fealty to his lord should always remember these six things: uninjured, safe, honest, useful, easy, possible. Uninjured, that is, that he not harm his lord bodily. Safe, that he not harm him concerning his secret or the fortifications by which he can be safe. Honest, that he not harm him in his justice or in other matters which seem to concern his honor. Useful, that he not damage his possessions. Easy or possible, that that good which his lord could do easily not be made hard for him, and lest that which was possible be rendered impossible. Now it is just that the faithful man (*fidelis*) avoid these harmful things, but the oath is not thereby merited; for it is not enough to abstain from evil, unless he do what is good.

So it remains that in the same six aforesaid things he faithfully do counsel and aid [*consilium et auxilium*] to his lord, if he wishes to seem worthy of a benefice and to be secure in the fealty he has sworn. Also the lord ought to reciprocate to his faithful man in all these things. If he does not, he shall rightly be deemed perfidious, just as he who is caught in transgression either by doing or by consenting is perfidious and perjured.

I should have written you more if I were not occupied with much else, especially with the restoration of the city and our church, all of which recently burned in an appalling fire. Although for a little while we cannot help but be shaken by this injury, nevertheless we revive in the hope of God's solace and yours.

*From *Recueil des historiens des Gaules et de la France*, X (Paris, 1874), 463. Translated by ed.

C. *Counsel, Aid and Urban Deputations in an Early Provincial Assembly in France: The "General Court" of Agenais (1182; c. 1221–c. 1240)**

1. (1182) And when the prince of the land or his seneschal[2] shall convoke his general court, some or all of the consuls, according to the lord's order, should go to the said court for the town of Marmande at the expense of the town. When the prince of the land or his seneschal shall order his army in Agenais, the consuls of the town should go in that army. . . .

2. (c. 1221–c. 1240) And the men of Agen henceforth are not required . . . to do military service against any one or ones unless in the diocese of Agenais and [unless?] as aforesaid, they will do right according to the jurisdiction of the lord and of his court, which court should be [composed] of the barons and knights of Agenais and of the consuls and good men of the city of Agen and of the towns of Agenais. . . .

D. *Royal Engagements to a* Cortes *Including Town Deputies at Leon (1188)***

In the name of God. I, the lord Alfonso king of Leon and of Galicia, when I celebrated court at Leon with the archbishop and bishops and magnates of my kingdom and with the citizens elected by each city, have established and confirmed under oath that, to all men of my kingdom, clergy as well as lay persons, I would preserve their good customs constituted by my predecessors.

. . . I have promised, moreover, that I shall not make war or peace or treaty unless with the counsel of bishops, nobles and good men, by whose counsel I ought to be ruled. . . .

E. *Counsel and Consent in Canon Law (twelfth century)****

1. Gratian, *Decretum*, XII, ii, c. 52: Without exception we decree that no bishop give or presume to exchange or sell anything of his church's property unless

---

*1. From the customs of Marmande, Archives nationales, JJ. 72, fol. 150v, translated by editor.—2. From the customs of Agen, H. Tropamer, *La coutume d'Agen* (Bordeaux, 1911) p. 28, translated by editor.

**From *Córtes de los antiguos reinos de Leon y de Castilla*, I (Madrid, 1861), 39-40. Translated by editor.

***Selections translated by editor. That from Huguccio is based on G. I. Langmuir's quotation (see above, p. 115) from Bibliotheque nationale, ms. latin 15396, verified in Munich, ms. latin 10247.

perhaps he do one of these things for the sake of improvement and decide that with the consultation and consent of all the clergy, that there be no doubt of its advantage to the church.

2. Huguccio of Pisa, *Summa*, to (*Decretum*) XII, ii, c. 52, on the word "consultation" (*tractatu*): This is said to prevent fraud, because they might be convoked without their counsel being taken. But having at once notified them of the matter, the bishop might proceed in the matter without their counsel, and so he says that he ought to treat the matter by their counsel. For the summons does not alone suffice unless he not only consults them but receives their counsel. . . . And because they might disagree he adds "with consent"; and because two might consent and all others disagree, he adds "of all."

F. *National Counsel and Taxation: The English* Magna Carta *of 1215**

(Chapter 12) Let no scutage or aid be imposed in our kingdom unless by the common counsel [*commune consilium*] of our kingdom, except in order to ransom our body, to knight our eldest son and to marry once our eldest daughter; and for these let there be only a reasonable aid. Let it be done likewise with the aids of the city of London.

(Chapter 14) And for having the common counsel of the kingdom to assess aid other than in the three aforesaid cases or to assess scutage, we shall cause to be summoned archbishops, bishops, abbots, counts and the greater barons individually by our letter; and besides we shall have summoned generally, by our sheriffs and bailiffs, all those who hold directly from us: for a certain day, with at least forty days' notice, and a specified place; and in all letters of that summons we shall explain the cause of summons; and when the summons has thus been made, let the business proceed on the assigned day according to the counsel of those present even if not all those summoned should come.

G. *Parliaments According to the Provisions of Oxford (1258)***

Of the parliaments, how many shall be held annually, and in what manner.

It is to be remembered that the twenty-four have ordained that there be three parliaments a year. The first at the octave of St. Michael. The second the morrow of Candlemas. The third the first day of June, to wit, three weeks before St. John's day. To these three parliaments the elected councillors of the king shall come, even

---

*From the *Magna Carta* of 1215, as edited by William Stubbs, *Select Charters* . . . , 9th ed., revised by H. W. C. Davis (Oxford, 1913), pp. 294-295. Translated by editor.

**From William Stubbs, *Select Charters,* 9th ed., p. 387 (translated from the French).

if they are not sent for, to see the state of the realm, and to treat of the common wants of the kingdom, and of the king in like manner. And at other times in like manner when occasion shall be, by the king's command.

So it is to be remembered that the commonalty shall elect twelve honest men, who shall come to the parliaments and at other times when occasion shall be, when the king or his council shall send for them, to treat of the wants of the king and of the kingdom. And that the commonalty shall hold as established that which these twelve shall do. And that shall be done to spare the cost of the commonalty. . . .

H. *Summons to the Parliament of 1265 (14 December 1264)**

Henry, by the grace of God king of England, lord of Ireland and duke of Aquitaine, to the venerable father in Christ Robert, by the same grace bishop of Dunwich, greeting. When our dearest and eldest son Edward, after the gravely divisive disturbances that formerly troubled our realm, made himself security for assuring and confirming peace in our realm, and since, with God's blessing, the aforesaid disturbance has now been quieted; for salubrious deliberation about this and for the full securing of peace and tranquillity for the honor of God and the confirming and perfecting of the utility of all our realm, and for certain other matters of our realm which we do not wish to pursue without your counsel and that of our other prelates and magnates, it is fitting for us to consult them; we order you, asking in the faith and devotion by which you are bound to us, that, setting aside all other events and business, you come to us at London on the octaves of next Saint Hilary,[3] to discuss and give counsel on the aforesaid [matters] with us and with the aforesaid prelates and magnates. And do this without fail, as you love us and our honor and yours and the common tranquillity of our kingdom. Witness the king at Worcester on the 14th day of December.

Likewise it is directed to each sheriff in England that he cause to come to the king at London, on the aforesaid octaves in prescribed form, two knights from among the more legal, upright and discreet knights of each shire.

Likewise in the prescribed form it is written to the citizens of York, the citizens of Lincoln, and to the other towns of England, that they send in the prescribed way two of the more discreet, legal and upright citizens or townsmen. . . .

*From William Stubbs, *Select Charters,* 9th ed., pp. 403-404. Translated by editor.

I. Humbert of Romans, *On the Erudition of Preachers*
Ch. 86 *In the Parliaments of Kings**

It should be noted that it is customary among great kings to hold parliaments each year at certain times, in which convene many counsellors and many secular magnates and many prelates. Now such parliaments are held for three principal reasons: namely, that the greater matters which cannot easily be settled during the year may there more wisely be despatched with greater deliberation, because greater things should be reserved for greater deliberation, as is said in *Exodus* 18;[4] also, that account may be rendered there by the king's agents, according to that in *Matthew* 18: "The kingdom of heaven is like the human king who wished to account with his servants;"[5] and, again, that there may be ordained what is necessary for the kingdom, according to that in 1 Machabees: "It is my duty to ordain for the kingdom."[6]

Now for choosing subjects of predication in such parliaments, assuming a suitable audience, it should be noted that many things to be opposed by preachers generally occur in such parliaments. One is the wickedness of counsellors. For there are counsellors of kings who sometimes, in order to please them [the kings], fashion their counsels according to their sense of the king's pleasure. Sometimes they turn away from the right on account of hatred or friendship for certain people, or for like reasons, and give bad counsels; and this is most dangerous in a kingdom, for as a certain wise man said: "More easily does the king bend to his counsellors than they to him," and so it is more damaging for the republic to have bad counsellors near the king than a bad king . . . . Another is perversity of judgment. . . . Another is the difficulty of obtaining justice . . . . Another is the abasement of the poor. For they are so excluded and scorned in such courts that they can scarcely obtain a hearing . . . . Another is the defense of bad men . . . . Another is corruption by gifts, which today corrupt almost all courts . . . .

*From Humbert of Romans, *De eruditione praedicatorum*, ed. Marguerin de La Bigne, *Maxima bibliotheca veterum patrum* . . . , XXV (Lyons, 1677), 559-560. Translated by editor.

J. *Summonses to the Parliament of November 1295 (30 September to 3 October 1295)**

1. (Summons of archbishop and clergy) The king to the venerable father in Christ Robert, by the same grace archbishop of Canterbury, primate of all England, greeting. As a most just law ordained by the provident circumspection of sacred princes urges and establishes that what touches all should be approved by all, so is it most evident that common dangers should be met by remedies commonly established. Verily you know well enough, as is now divulged, we believe, in all regions of the world, how the king of France has deceived us fraudulently and cunningly in respect to our land of Gascony, wickedly keeping it from us. Now, moreover, not content with the aforesaid fraud and wickedness, having gathered a large fleet and a copious multitude of warriors to invade our realm . . . , he proposes to destroy altogether the English tongue if there be power sufficient to the detestable plan of iniquity—which may God avert! Therefore, since darts foreseen injure less and your fortunes, like those of the other citizens of the same kingdom, are greatly concerned in this affair, we order you in the faith and devotion by which you are bound to us, firmly enjoining that on the Sunday next after the feast of Saint Martin in Winter[7] you be present in person at Westminster, first notifying the prior and chapter of your church, the archdeacons and all the clergy of your diocese, causing the said prior and archdeacons to be present together with you in their own persons, and the said chapter by one, and the same clergy by two, suitable proctors having full and sufficient power from the same chapter and clergy, then and there in all ways to treat, ordain and do with us and with the other prelates and magnates and other inhabitants of our realm, whatever may be required to counter such dangers and cogitated evils. Witness the king at Wengham on the thirtieth day of September.

(Similar letters were sent, with appropriate changes, to the archbishop of York and the other bishops; and, omitting the clause "first notifying," to 67 abbots, the masters of the Temple and of Sempringham, and the prior of the Hospital.)

2. (Summons of barons) The king to his beloved and faithful kinsman Edmund, earl of Cornwall, greeting. Because we wish to have colloquium and discussion with you and with other leading men of our kingdom regarding remedies to be provided against the dangers which threaten our whole realm these days, we order you, enjoining firmly in the faith and devotion by which you are bound to us, that on the Sunday next after the feast of St. Martin in the coming winter, you appear in person at Westminster to discuss, ordain and do with us and with the prelates and other great men and other inhabitants of our realm, whatever may be required to counter such dangers. Witness the king at Canterbury on the first day of October.

(Similar letters were sent to 7 earls and 41 barons.)

*From William Stubbs, *Select Charters*, 9th ed., pp. 480-482.

3. (Summons to shires and towns) The king to the sheriff of Northampton. Because we wish to have colloquium and discussion with the earls, barons and other magnates of our realm regarding remedies . . . and accordingly have directed them to be with us on the Sunday . . . ; we firmly order you, enjoining that you cause to be elected without delay two knights from the aforesaid county and two citizens from each city of that county, and two burghers from each borough, from among the more discreet and capable of work, and that you have them come to us at the aforesaid time and place; in such a way that the said knights have full and sufficient power for themselves and the community of the aforesaid shire, and the said citizens and burghers for themselves and the community of cities and boroughs separately, to do, then and there, what shall be ordained by common counsel in the aforesaid matters; so that the aforesaid business shall not remain unfinished in any way for lack of such power. And you are to have there the names of the knights, citizens and burghers, and this writ. Witness the king at Canterbury on the third day of October.

K. *Order to Collect the Aid Granted in the Parliament of November 1295 (4 December 1295)**

The king to the knights and free tenants and all the community of Rutlandshire, greeting. Since the earls, barons, knights and others of our realm have now, in aid of our war, as formerly to us and our ancestors, the kings of England, freely granted an eleventh of all their moveable goods; and the citizens, burghers and other good men of our domains, cities and boroughs of the same realm have courteously and freely granted a seventh of all their moveable goods, except for those things that were excluded from the last tenth granted to us; we, wishing to provide for the levy and collection of the aforesaid eleventh and seventh with the least injury and trouble for the people of our said realm, have assigned our beloved and faithful Robert of Flixthorpe and John of Wakerle . . . , or either one of them whenever, when one of them is prevented by serious illness, they cannot both be present, to assess, tax, levy, and collect the said eleventh and seventh in the aforesaid shire, to bring [the money] to our Exchequer, and deposit it there at the following terms: namely, one-half by the next feast of the Purification of St. Mary,[8] and the other half by the feast of the following Pentecost.[9] And so we direct you that you be helpful, and responsive to the aforesaid Robert and John in the aforesaid matters, advising and aiding them, inasmuch as they will speak for us. Witness the king at Westminster on the fourth day of December.

L. *Procedure in an Assembly at Paris (1 August 1314)***

(This text is quoted by Robert Fawtier in the selection printed above, p. 79.)

M. *Summons to a* Cort *at Montblanch (Catalonia), to be Held on 11 April 1333 (11 March 1333)****

Alfonso,[10] etc., to his faithful counselors, good men and community of the city of Barcelona, greeting, etc. Because for the arduous business and dangers of the wars threatening our domain by land and sea we regard your counsel and aid necessary to oppose and resist the aforesaid swiftly, and on this account we have summoned the Catalans to court in the town of Montblanch; therefore we tell you

---

*From William Stubbs, *Select Charters*, 9th ed., p. 482. Translated by editor.

**From *Les Grandes Chroniques de France*, ed. Jules Viard, VIII (Paris, 1934), 299-301.

****Córtes de los antiguos reinos de Aragón y de Valencia y principado de Cataluña*, I[2] (Madrid, 1896), 294. Translated by editor.

and command that you ordain and constitute your suitable syndics or proctors, whom you are to cause to appear with full and sufficient power on the eighth day after the coming feast of the pascal resurrection of the Lord in the said town of Montblanch to discuss and ordain and confirm with us together with others of the court whatever may be opportune about the matters aforesaid. Given at Barcelona on the fifth Ides of March in the year of the Lord 1332.[11]

(Letters of summons in the same form were sent to the archbishop of Tarragona, six bishops, seven cathedral chapters, nineteen abbots, the military orders, forty barons, thirty-seven knights, and seventeen other towns.)

N. *Summons to an Assembly at Paris to be Held on 2 February 1346 (4 January 1346)**

Philip,[12] etc., to our beloved and faithful [such and such]. We have learned from trustworthy persons that our subjects and our people are so troubled by impositions, *gabelles* and charges that have been made because of our wars, and also . . . that our sergeants and commissioners sent through our kingdom for many and diverse reasons have greatly and excessively multiplied, wherefore we feel great compassion and very great dissatisfaction at heart and would willingly provide for as good and agreeable remedies as we can. And so to determine what best and most expediently to do, we have ordered that the counsel and opinion of prelates, clergymen, barons and other nobles [and] of the communes and good towns of our realm be taken on this matter. So we order and require that, setting aside all excuses, you be before us at Paris on the day of the next Candlemas—provided, that is, that you do not go at the summons of our very dear son the duke of Normandy,[13] who is at Toulouse on that same day—in order to give us the best advice you can on the aforesaid things, so that by the good counsel of you and our other subjects whom we summon for that day we may ordain on this matter as may be agreeable to God and profitable to our people and to all our kingdom. Given at St-Ouen-les-St.-Denis on the fourth day of January in the year 1345.[14]

---

* Archives nationales, P. 2291, fols. 663-664. Translated by editor.

Notes

1. *Ecclesiasticus* xxxii:24.
2. The prince of the land was (then) the Duke of Aquitaine, Richard the Lion-Heart; the seneschal was his chief deputy.
3. 20 January 1265.—Ed.
4. See *Exodus* 18:22.—Ed.
5. *Matthew* 18:23.—Ed.
6. Cf. 1 Machabees 6:57.—Ed.
7. I.e., on 13 November 1295.
8. 2 February 1296.
9. 12 May 1296.
10. Alfonso IV of Aragon (1327-1336).
11. 11 March 1333 (new style).
12. Philip VI (1328-1350).
13. John, later king (1350-1364).
14. 1346 (new style).

Suggestions for Further Reading

No single work adequately surveys the literature, much less the history, of medieval representative institutions. The bibliography appended to C. H. McIlwain's "Medieval Estates" in the *Cambridge Medieval History*, vii (Cambridge, 1932), though somewhat dated, is full and useful for its reference to basic collections of sources as well as to the older standard works. Less full but more up-to-date is the bibliography in A. Marongiu, *Medieval Parliaments: a Comparative Study*, tr. S. J. Woolf (London, 1968). See also H. M. Cam, A. Marongiu and G. Stökl, "Recent Work and Present Views on the Origins and Development of Representative Assemblies," *Relazioni del X Congresso di Scienze Storiche*, i (Florence, 1955).

Among comparative surveys, McIlwain's chapter has not been superseded, although one should now also read B. Guenèe, *L'Occident aux XIVe et XVe siècles. Les États* (Paris, 1971); for the continent, R. Fawtier, *L'Europe occidentale de 1270 à 1380*, pt 1 (Paris, 1940) is excellent. Other useful treatments are by E. P. Cheyney,

The Dawn of a New Era, 1250-1453 (New York, 1936), ch. 3, and R. H. Lord, "The Parliaments of the Middle Ages and the Early Modern Period," *Catholic Historical Review*, xvi (1930), 125-144 (and in Bobbs-Merrill reprints). *La société d'Ancien Régime*, 2d ed. (Louvain, 1952) by Émile Lousse is not only the outstanding single work in the corporatist school but necessarily eschews national boundaries, referring to an enormous specialized literature. The *Studies presented to the International Commission for the History of Representative and Parliamentary Institutions*, presently close to forty volumes (since 1937), include not only corporatist, but national, local, theoretical, and ecclesiastical studies ranging far beyond the European Middle Ages.

On the origins of representative institutions as a general historical problem (beyond works already cited), see H. Spangenberg, *Vom Lehnstaat zum Ständestaat* (Munich, 1912); F. Kern, *Kingship and Law in the Middle Ages*, tr. S. B. Chrimes (Oxford, 1939); M. V. Clarke, *Medieval Representation and Consent...* (London, 1936); and the articles by T. N. Bisson and B. Tierney abridged in this collection. The contribution of the Roman and canon laws to representation in assemblies is stressed by Gaines Post in articles published in *Speculum* (1943) and *Traditio* (1943, 1946); these are reprinted in his *Studies in Medieval Legal Thought...* (Princeton, 1964), chs. 2-4. For ecclesiastical theories of consultation, see B. Tierney, *Foundations of the Conciliar Theory...* (Cambridge, 1955). Ernest Barker, *The Dominican Order and Convocation* (Oxford, 1913) is a stimulating if unpersuasive argument for clerical influence on secular representation; see also H. P. Tunmore, "The Dominican Order and Parliament: an Unsolved Problem in the History of Representation," *Catholic Historical Review*, xxvi (1941), 479-489. On parliamentarism in relation to the state, see G. de Lagarde, *La naissance de l'esprit laïque*, new ed., 5 vols. (Paris, 1956-70); O. Brunner, "Moderner Verfassungsbegriff und mittelalterlicher Verfassungsgeschichte," *Mitteilungen des Instituts für österreichische Geschichtsforschung*, xiv (1939); J. R. Strayer, *On the Medieval Origins of the Modern State* (Princeton, 1970).

From the enormous literature on the English parliament, only a few more works can be mentioned. A. F. Pollard's *The Evolution of Parliament* (London, 1920; 2d ed., 1926) is a brilliant survey not altogether dated by recent work. May McKisack, *The Parliamentary Representation of the English Boroughs during the Middle Ages* (Oxford, 1932) is solid. G. L. Haskins, with some other American scholars, has stressed fiscal reasons for the summons of representatives to parliament; his *The Growth of English Representative Government* (Philadelphia, 1948) is very readable. A variety of problems are dealt with by G. T. Lapsley, *Crown, Community and Parliament in the Later Middle Ages* (Oxford, 1951); B. Wilkinson, *Constitutional History of England, 1216-1399*, 3 vols. (London, 1948-58); and diverse writers in *Historical Studies of the English Parliament*, ed. E. B. Fryde and E. Miller, 2 vols. (Cambridge, 1970). Good recent reviews of the literature are E. Miller, *The Origins of Parliament* (Historical Association, 1960); J. G. Edwards,

Historians and the Medieval English Parliament (Glasgow, 1960); and G. P. Cuttino, "Medieval Parliament Reinterpreted," *Speculum*, xli (1966), 681-687.

For France, one may get an idea of the older literature from P. Viollet, *Histoire des institutions politiques et administratives de la France*, 3 vols. (Paris, 1890-1903), iii, ch. 6, and F. Lot and R. Fawtier, *Histoire des institutions françaises*, ii (Paris, 1958), livre 6. On early royal consultation, see now G. I. Langmuir, "Counsel and Capetian Assemblies," cited and excerpted above; "Concilia and Capetian Assemblies, 1179-1230," *Album Helen Maud Cam*, ii (*Studies presented to the Internat. Commission . . . Representative . . . Institutions*, xxiv, Louvain, 1961), 27-63; and "Politics and Parliaments in the early Thirteenth Century," *Études présentées à la Commission intern. pour l'histoire des assemblées d'États*, xxix, Paris, 1966), 47-62. See also T. N. Bisson, "Consultative Functions in the King's Parlements (1250-1314)," *Speculum*, xliv (1969), 353-373; and articles by C. H. Taylor in *Speculum* for years 1936, 1938, 1939, 1954, and 1968. For consent to French taxation, see J. R. Strayer and C. H. Taylor, *Studies in Early French Taxation* (Cambridge, M., 1939), and J. B. Henneman, Jr., *Royal Taxation in Fourteenth Century France, 1322-1356* (Princeton, 1971). Early provincial consultation is examined in T. N. Bisson, *Assemblies and Representation in Languedoc in the Thirteenth Century* (Princeton, 1964). Among the better monographs on the provincial Estates, are those by A. Thomas (on central France, 1879); L. Cadier (Béarn, 1888); C. Hirschauer (Artois, 1923); H. Prentout (Normandy, 1925-27); H. Gilles (Languedoc, 1965); and J. Dhondt, "Les origines des États de Flandre," *Anciens Pays et Assemblées d'États* (Louvain, 1950), 1-52.

For the Spanish realms, one may consult R. B. Merriman, "The Cortes of the Spanish Kingdoms," *American Historical Review*, xvi (1911), 476-495, who cites the older literature. More recently, historians have studied the transformation of the *curia* into representative bodies and the introduction of urban deputations: see C. Sanchez-Albornoz, *La curia regia portuguesa: siglos XII y XIII* (Madrid, 1920); E. S. Procter, "The Development of the Catalan *Corts* in the Thirteenth Century," *Homenatge a Antoni Rubio i Lluch*, 3 vols. (Barcelona, 1936), iii, 525-546; J. F. O'Callaghan, "The Beginning of the Cortes of Leon-Castile," *American Historical Review*, lxxiv (1969), 1503-1537.

For the Empire and Italy, see G. Ermini, *I parlamenti dello stato della chiesa dalle origini al periodo Albornoziano* (Bologna, 1930); P. Leicht, "L'introduction des villes dans les assemblées d'États en Italie," *Bulletin of the International Commission of the Historical Sciences*, ix (1937), 419-424, and "La posizione giuridica dei parlamenti medievali italiani," *Études présentées à la Commission internat . . . Histoire des Assemblées d'États* (Louvain, 1937), 91-109; G. Barraclough, *The Origins of Modern Germany*, 2d ed. (Oxford, 1947), pp. 325-352; C. C. Bayley, *The Formation of the German College of Electors in the Mid-Thirteenth Century* (Toronto, 1949); and J. Gernhüber, *Die Landfriedensbewegung in Deutschland bis zum Mainzer Reichslandfrieden von 1235* (Bonn, 1952); as well as A. Marongiu, *Medieval Parliaments*.